The First Passage

BLACKS IN THE AMERICAS
1502–1617

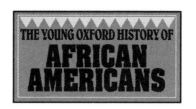

THE YOUNG OXFORD HISTORY OF
AFRICAN AMERICANS

Robin D. G. Kelley and Earl Lewis
General Editors

The First Passage

❖ ❖ ❖

BLACKS IN THE AMERICAS
1502-1617

COLIN A. PALMER

Oxford University Press
New York • Oxford

Oxford University Press

Oxford   New York
Athens Auckland Bangkok Bombay
Calcutta Cape Town Dar es Salaam Delhi
Florence Hong Kong Istanbul Karachi
Kuala Lumpur Madras Madrid Melbourne
Mexico City Nairobi Paris Singapore
Taipei Tokyo Toronto
and associated companies in
Berlin   Ibadan

Published by Oxford University Press, Inc.,
200 Madison Avenue, New York, New York 10016

Library of Congress Cataloging-in-Publication Data

Palmer, Colin A.
The first passage: Blacks in the Americas, 1502-1617 / Colin A. Palmer
p. cm. — (Young Oxford history of African Americans; vol. 1)
Includes bibliographical references and index.
1. Blacks—America—History—Juvenile literature. 2. Slavery—America—History—Juvenile literature.
3. Slave trade—History—Juvenile literature. 4. Afro-Americans—History—To 1863—Juvenile literature.
[1. Blacks—America—History. 2. Slavery—America—History. 3. Slave trade—History.
4. Afro-Americans—History—To 1863.]
I. Title. II. Series

E29.N3P35 1995   94-17355
973'. 0496073—dc20   CIP
                                                               AC

ISBN 0-19-508699-6 (lib. ed.); ISBN 0-19-509905-2 (trade ed.); 0-19-508502-7 (series, lib. ed.)

3 5 7 9 8 6 4 2

Printed in the United States of America
on acid-free paper

Design: Sandy Kaufman
Layout: Loraine Machlin
Picture research: Patricia Burns, Laura Kreiss

On the cover: The watercolor *Slave Deck of the Albanoz* was painted by an English officer of the ship during a voyage.
Frontispiece: Africans huddle aboard a slave ship during their voyage to the Americas.
Page 9: Detail from, *The Contribution of the Negro to Democracy in America,* (1943), by Charles White, 11'9" x 17'3."
Hampton University Museum, Hampton, Virginia.

Contents

ROBIN D.G. KELLEY
EARL LEWIS

INTRODUCTION

The history of African Americans begins on the African continent, a huge and varied land bounded by the Atlantic and Indian oceans. It was home to people with different languages, traditions, histories, and religions. They called themselves Twi, Yoruba, Ethiopian, Zulu, Ashanti, and Kumba, among other names. Some lived in large ancient kingdoms as old as the annals of recorded history, and others lived in small family groupings. Some worshiped one god, and others many gods. Some lived in societies headed by powerful men, and others in societies headed by powerful women.

Whether in cities or rural areas, whether Muslim, Christian, or of an indigenous religion, the peoples of this amazingly diverse continent had long played a central role in the affairs of the ancient world. Egyptian advances in medicine, language, and architecture greatly influenced the Greek and Roman worlds. Gold from the Bure and Bambuk goldfields of West Africa was traded with the Mediterranean world, where the accumulation of significant quantities enabled the merchants of Genoa (in Italy) to underwrite European exploration and expansion. Likewise, notable centers of learning such as Timbuktu attracted visitors from Europe and the Orient and their scholarship greatly enriched the Islamic world.

The roles of Africans in world affairs changed significantly with the rise of the South Atlantic system (the slave trade and the resulting slave-based economy). As European explorers made their way to the Americas beginning in the 15th century, they expected to find streets paved with gold. The Americas were indeed rich in natural resources, but the bounty had to be excavated, cultivated, and processed. Labor was needed. After experimenting with slave labor on sugar plantations in the Mediterranean region and off the coast of West Africa, and after unsuccessfully trying Indian labor in Brazil, the Portuguese settlers turned to African labor for the sugar industry there.

What followed was the forced migration and enslavement of several million Africans of varied ethnic backgrounds. Although scholars debate the exact numbers, it is understood that somewhere between 10 and 20 million people became part of the system of enslavement that ultimately led to the making of an African-American diaspora, a geographically dispersed community of African peoples. The process of creating this diaspora also involved transforming many different African peoples into African Americans. Many died in the trek from the interior to the coast of Africa, others during the wait for a slave ship to take them to the Americas, and scores of others during the harsh Middle Passage. Out of the crucible of their suffering was forged a new people—no longer simply Twi, Yoruba, Ashanti, or Kumba. In the Americas, they first became Africans and then African Americans. This process of people making is a central feature of African-American history.

This book examines that process. It explores the variety of social, political, cultural, and economic institutions and practices in ancient and medieval Africa. It asks questions about family patterns, religious beliefs, social organization, and economic involvement. The book also addresses the thorny subject of slavery on the African continent. It then tells the story of the Middle Passage and outlines the world that enslaved Africans built in Brazil and Mexico in the 15th and 16th centuries.

This book is part of an 11-volume series that narrates African-American history from the 15th through the 20th centuries. Since the 1960s, a rapid explosion in research on black Americans has significantly modified previous understanding of that experience. Studies of slavery, African-American culture, social protest, families, and religion, for example, silenced those who had previously labeled black Americans insignificant historical actors. This new research followed a general upsurge of interest in the social and cultural experiences of the suppos-edly powerless men and women who did not control the visible reins of power. The result has been a careful and illuminating portrait of how ordinary people make history and serve as the architects of their own destinies.

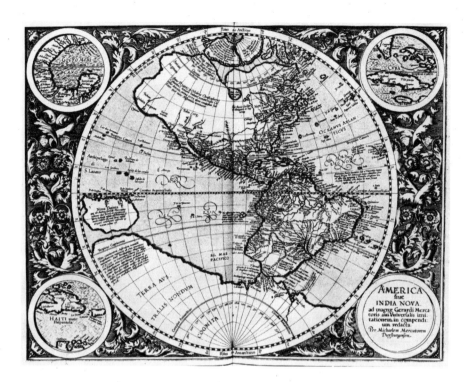

A 1595 map of the Americas published in the Mercator Atlas. *In both North and South America, Africans forged new communities and identities.*

This series explores many aspects of the lives of African Americans. It describes how blacks shaped and changed the history of this nation. It also places the lives of African Americans in the context of the Americas as a whole. We start the story more than a century before the day in 1619 when 19 "negars" stepped off a Spanish ship in Jamestown, Virginia, and end with the relationship between West Indian immigrants and African Americans in large urban centers like New York in the late 20th century.

At the same time, the series addresses a number of interrelated questions: What was life like for the first Africans to land in the Americas, and what were the implications for future African Americans? Were all Africans and African Americans enslaved? How did race shape slavery and how did slavery influence racism? The series also considers questions about male-female relationships, the forging of African-American communities, religious beliefs and practices, the experiences of the young, and the changing nature of social protest. The key events in American history are here, too, but viewed from the perspective of African Americans. The result is a fascinating and compelling story of nearly five centuries of African-American history.

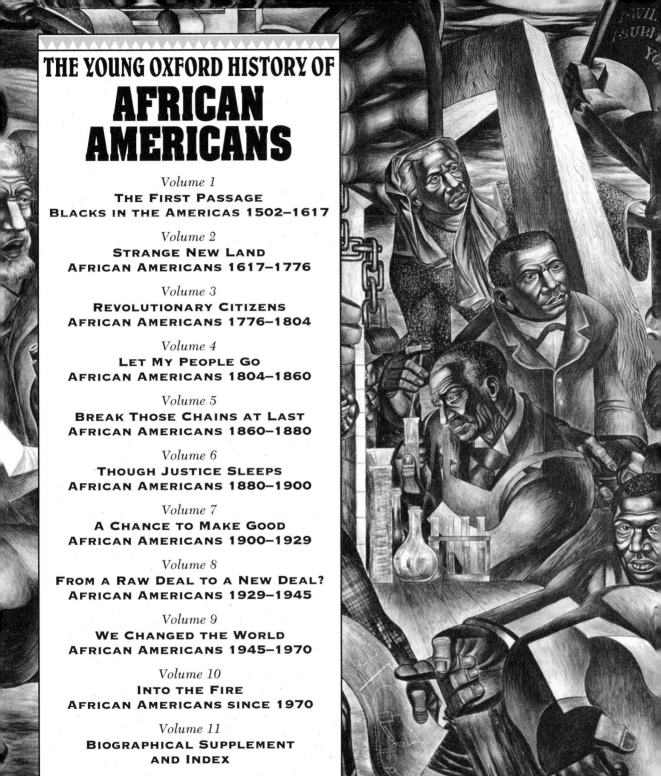

THE YOUNG OXFORD HISTORY OF
AFRICAN AMERICANS

BLACKS IN A NEW LAND

W ithout exception, the contemporary societies of North and South America and the Caribbean include peoples of African descent. They form the numerical majority in the Caribbean, are about one half of Brazil's population, and make up a significant minority in the United States. In other countries, such as Canada, Mexico, Venezuela, and Colombia, blacks are present in smaller numbers. Regardless of the societies in which they live, these peoples share a common historical origin and ancestral homeland. Their experiences in the Americas have also been remarkably similar since the 16th century, when they began to arrive from Africa in ever-increasing numbers.

This book is about the first century of the recorded black presence in the Americas. Black Africans were brought as slaves into the Caribbean islands and the mainland colonies of Central and South America, first by the Spaniards and later by the Portuguese. Beginning in 1502, the slave trade gathered momentum as white colonists came to rely on this forced black labor. During the early years of the trade, Africans passed through Spain (where many remained) to the Americas. By 1518, however, a direct trade route from Africa to the Americas was introduced.

This book chronicles the experiences of these first Africans and the roles they played in laying the foundations of the new societies in the Americas. It follows the history of these peoples by looking at their lives

A 16th-century bronze sculpture of the Queen Mother of Benin, a powerful African kingdom well-known for its bronze plaques and sculptures.

11

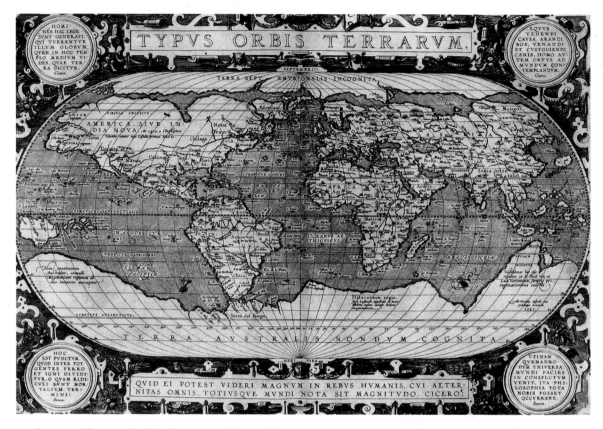

in the Caribbean islands of Hispaniola (modern Haiti and the Dominican Republic), Jamaica, Cuba, and Puerto Rico. Mexico, Peru, and to some extent, Brazil, receive fuller treatment because of their larger populations and because more research has been done on the history of blacks in those societies in the 16th century. The book looks at other Spanish American colonies, such as Colombia, Venezuela, and Argentina, only in passing. They had tiny black populations in the 16th century, and much research remains to be done on the black presence in those colonies.

This book focuses on the nature of the Africans' journey to the Americas, their place in the colonial societies, and their position as exploited workers. It also examines their struggle to create and sustain social institutions, such as the family, to give meaning to their lives, and their efforts to liberate themselves and destroy slavery.

Not all Africans in the Americas, even in the 16th century, served as slaves for the duration of their lives. Some managed to achieve their freedom; others were born free. In 1617 the first town or settlement

This world map, printed in 1587, provided the most accurate representation to date of the coastlines of the Americas. Africans were first shipped to the Americas as slaves in 1502.

12

controlled by free blacks in the Americas was established in Mexico. This was a major development in black life in the Western Hemisphere; it was the first time that a group of Africans gained the right to live as free people. These pioneers had successfully thrown off the yoke of slavery through their own efforts, setting the stage for the eventual liberation of other enslaved Africans. But almost three centuries passed before this goal would be accomplished everywhere in the Americas.

Two years after this free Mexican town—San Lorenzo de los Negros—received its charter, about 20 Africans disembarked from a Dutch ship at Jamestown, Virginia. These people were the first Africans shipped to the new and permanent settlement that the English colonists had established in North America. They came 117 years after Africans were first enslaved in the Americas, in Hispaniola.

This book does not deal with the history of the Africans who arrived at Jamestown. It ends in 1617, just as freedom beckoned for a few Africans in Mexico, and slavery was about to be introduced into the English North American colonies. As with the case of the enslaved people in the Caribbean and Latin America, the Africans who landed at Jamestown had to struggle to maintain their human dignity and create their own space in alien lands.

CHAPTER 1
FROM AFRICA TO THE AMERICAS

I n the 1780s, Olaudah Equiano sat down to write his memoirs. The story that he had to tell was fascinating, deeply moving, and a testimony to the ability of human beings to confront and overcome seemingly impossible odds. Equiano was an African who had been forcibly taken from his homeland and enslaved in the Americas. He eventually achieved his freedom and became a leader in the antislavery movement in England. Equiano's experiences were similar, in many respects, to those of the millions of African-born peoples who were enslaved in the Americas both before and after he wrote his autobiography.

Equiano was born in 1745 in what is now Nigeria. He recalled that he was kidnapped by slave traders when he was only 11 years old. "One day, when all of our people were gone out to their works as usual," he wrote, "and only I and my dear sister were left to mind the house, two men and a woman got over our walls, and in a moment seized us both; and, without giving us time to cry out, or make resistance, they stopped our mouths, and ran off with us into the nearest wood." Over the next several months, the terrified boy, now separated from his sister, was sold to several different traders. When he was finally brought on board a slave ship bound for the Americas, he remembered seeing "a multitude of black people of every description chained together, every one of their

Olaudah Equiano, shown here in an engraving printed in his 1789 autobiography, was captured by slave traders when he was 11 years old. Equiano's autobiography describes his experiences as a slave in North America and the Caribbean and his successful efforts to purchase his freedom.

countenances expressing dejection and sorrow, I no longer doubted of my own fate; and, quite overpowered with horror and anguish, I fell motionless on the deck and fainted."

Equiano survived the journey to the Americas and was enslaved in Virginia and Barbados. One of his masters took him to London and renamed him Gustavus Vasa. In 1763 Equiano was taken from London to the West Indies and once again sold. He was purchased by a merchant who lived in Philadelphia. The enterprising young man did not lose confidence in himself or give up hope that he would eventually gain his freedom. Working for a wage in his spare time, he saved his earnings and purchased his freedom in 1766. Abandoning the Americas, Equiano sailed for England and worked at various jobs for the next several years. Not surprisingly, he participated in the antislavery movement, believing that "when you make men slaves you deprive them of half their virtue, you set them in your own conduct an example of fraud, [plunder], and cruelty and compel them to live with you in a state of war."

Equiano published his autobiography, *The Interesting Narrative of the Life of Olaudah Equiano, or Gustavus Vasa, the African,* in 1789. His remarkable book described the African homeland that he remembered, and it remains a classic account of slavery and the slave trade as seen through the eyes of someone who had become human property. When Equiano was kidnapped in 1756, the peoples of Africa had already been enslaved in the Americas for 243 years. Like Equiano, these people had brought memories of their homelands with them. They had all come from a continent with a richly diverse history and culture.

Modern archaeological research has established that Africa was the birthplace of human life. No precise date can be given for the emergence of early humans, or the hominid species, but it may have taken place about 2 million years ago. The earliest of these hominid fossils were discovered at Lake Turkana in Kenya, at Olduvai Gorge in Tanzania, and the river Omo in Ethiopia. Consequently, it is possible to claim that east and northeast Africa formed the cradle of human society. In time, over hundreds of thousands of years, early humans moved to other parts of Africa and to other continents.

The first Africans were nomadic peoples who made simple stone tools to aid them in their struggles for survival. With the passage of time, these tools became more sophisticated. The hand ax, for example,

A female hominid skull from Olduvai Gorge. Through their study of the fossils of early humans, archaeologists have concluded that human life began in Africa.

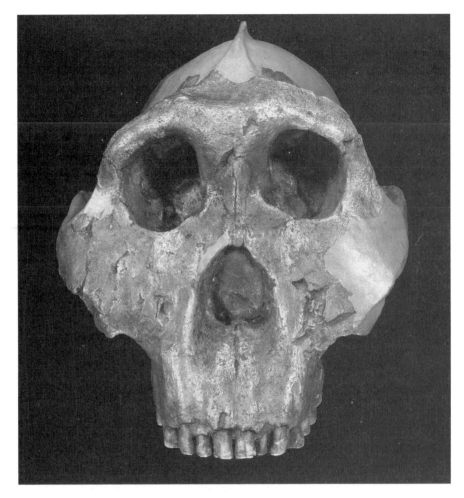

appeared around a million years ago. Its sharp cutting edges were more effective in the killing of prey than the earlier tools. Probably about 60,000 years ago, Africans started using fire. This development meant that meat could be cooked, and fire may even have been used to clear land for settlement or other purposes.

Human life in Africa, or elsewhere for that matter, was always changing. The people developed new tools, moved around, and organized their lives and societies in a variety of ways. There was much diversity among the African peoples in terms of their culture and skin color. In northeastern Africa, for example, the people tended to be lighter in complexion than those who lived in the tropical areas. Much of this difference in skin color was a result of living in different climates. Individuals who lived in areas of intense heat and sunlight developed the kind of dark skin pigmentation that allowed them to survive. Black skin provides a more effective protection against the ravages of intense heat than does lighter skin.

The black peoples of Africa, however, should not be characterized as belonging to a single race. In fact, many scholars have abandoned the use of the concept of "race" as a way of categorizing peoples. Skin color and other physical features do not reveal much about the genetic makeup of an individual or a group of individuals. Two individuals with the same skin color and hair texture may be more genetically different from one another than they are from two persons with another pigmentation. For this reason, scholars have concluded that Africans, and other peoples as well, are so internally different that the old way of classifying people according to physical appearance or "race" is no longer useful.

It is more useful to look at the African peoples according to language groupings. Different languages make up a family if their structures are basically similar. In most cases, the similarities in these languages result from the interaction among the speakers and the mutual borrowing of words. Using this method of studying languages, scholars have fitted the African peoples into five language families. These are the Afro-Asiatic family in North Africa, the Nilo-Saharan languages spoken in areas south and east of the Sahara and around the Nile River valley, the Congo-Kordofanian family spoken in West and West Central Africa, and the Khoisan group of languages spoken in southern Africa and parts of East Africa. A sixth family, the Austronesian, is found in Madagascar but is not native of Africa (having originated in Southeast Asia).

African societies varied in the pace of their development and the nature of the changes that they experienced over time. Egypt, for example, was the first society to begin cultivating food crops, probably about 5500 B.C. Other societies followed. By 3000 B.C., the people living in the savanna (grasslands) were producing a variety of grains and yams. The development of agriculture made it possible to support larger populations and contributed to the rise of settlements.

Throughout the continent, the people organized themselves in political units of various sizes and degrees of complexity. Egypt was the first great African civilization. Located in an area fertilized by the Nile,

This detail from a mural at the tomb of the Egyptian king Tutankhamen (1370–52 B.C.) shows warriors marching and driving chariots. Egypt was one of the early civilizations in Africa.

one of the great rivers of the world, Egypt made rapid strides in agriculture and commerce by 3000 B.C. Before 3100 B.C., however, several small states existed in the area. These political divisions came to an end when the states formed one kingdom ruled by the pharaohs. This national unity paved the way for an impressive civilization that would last for several centuries.

Egyptian civilization was characterized by a sophisticated hieroglyphic writing system, complex religious ideas, and impressive stone pyramids. Although historians disagree on this matter, it appears that the Egyptian peoples consisted of black Africans as well as lighter-skinned peoples from the Mediterranean area. Their civilization had a major impact on Greek culture and ultimately on Western civilization.

ANCIENT KINGDOMS OF THE WESTERN SUDAN

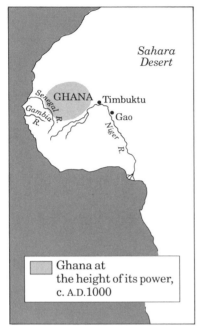

Ghana at
the height of its power,
c. A.D. 1000

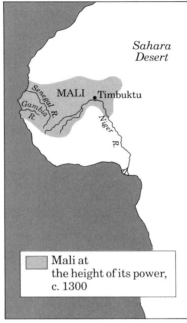

Mali at
the height of its power,
c. 1300

Songhai at
the height of its power,
c. early 16th century

Ancient Egypt is the best known of the early African societies, but it did not stand alone. Elsewhere, Africans developed a variety of states ranging from a few hundred people to large kingdoms and empires. These states were not all alike; there were variations in their political and social structures, the nature of the power exercised by the rulers, their religions, and so on. Many Africans believed that the authority and power of their ruler derived from the gods. Most of these societies had their own bureaucracies, taxation systems, and armed forces.

Some of the best-known states and empires were located in the western and central Sudan. Ghana, located in West Africa north of the Niger and Senegal valleys, was probably the earliest of them all. Noted for its great wealth and the power of its ruler, Ghana was said to have had an army of more than 200,000 soldiers around A.D. 1068. Later, the empire of Mali rose to prominence in the 14th century, occupying areas that are now part of Nigeria and the Guinea forests.

Mali's most famous ruler was Mansa Kankan Musa, who came to the throne in 1312. Bold and aggressive, he extended the frontiers of the Mali Empire to the Atlantic Ocean, incorporating several smaller states

In the western Sudan, the kingdom of Ghana was the first important African empire to emerge. The Mali Empire came to power in the 14th century and later, in the early 16th century, the Songhai kingdom dominated the region.

A detail from an early map of Africa shows Mali's emperor, Mansa Musa, holding a scepter and a glass ball. Under Mansa Musa's rule (1312–37), Mali greatly expanded its territory.

along the way. A Muslim, Mansa Musa undertook a pilgrimage to Mecca, which was then a part of Egypt, in 1324. On this journey, Mansa Musa made a lavish display of his wealth. He was accompanied by 500 slaves, each one bearing a staff of gold that weighed six pounds. In addition, 100 camels carried 30,000 pounds of gold. Mansa Musa's extravagance in Egypt created an accurate perception that his empire was one of the wealthiest then in existence.

The African peoples also developed cultural traditions that met their needs. The family was the basis of their social organization. Kinship ties, which united members of an ethnic group, were particularly strong. African societies were also deeply religious; most had a supreme god and other lesser deities. There was hardly any distinction between the religious and the secular, or civil, aspects of life. Religious beliefs determined when almost all activities, such as the planting seasons, harvest time, or the naming of children, would take place. Not surprisingly, the African peoples who came to the Americas brought very strong family and religious traditions with them.

African societies were never free from influences that originated outside of the continent. The Egyptian civilization enjoyed much interaction with the societies of the Mediterranean. There was a great deal of contact between the East African societies and those of Asia. Ethiopians had lived in Greece from about the 5th century B.C. Other Africans, usually traders, had visited various European countries for centuries.

In the 8th century, the new and aggressive Islamic religion began to gain converts in North and sub-Saharan Africa. With the embrace of Islam came important changes in the beliefs of the Africans and the nature of their legal systems. The Islamization of West Africa was aided by traders who converted to Islam in the north and brought their new religious ideas across the Sahara to the south. The pace of religious conversion and the number of converts varied, but few states remained untouched by Islam at the start of the Atlantic slave trade in the early 16th century. This did not mean, however, that most West Africans became Muslims and abandoned their traditional religious ideas. For many of the converts to Islam, ancient beliefs existed alongside the new ones, although these beliefs were undoubtedly modified in some way over time. Some of the Africans who were enslaved in the Americas were Muslims, but most were not.

Some scholars think that some West African peoples had established trading relationships with the native peoples of the Americas before the arrival of Columbus in 1492. Such contacts may have begun as early as the 7th century B.C. This conclusion is based on skeletal remains found in Central America that appear to be African, representations of African features in the art of some of the first Americans, as well as similarities in some African languages and those spoken in the Americas before Columbus. Because these kinds of evidence are subject to different interpretations, it cannot yet be established conclusively that Africans arrived in the Americas before the Europeans did.

Historians can never be certain of the number of Africans who were

This miniature Koran, the holy book of Islam, was made in northern Nigeria in the late 17th century. Islam began to spread through Africa in the 8th century, and the religion had an important effect on the beliefs and practices of many Africans.

brought to the Americas as slaves. Reliable records were often not kept, some have disappeared, and there is no firm data on those persons who were imported illegally. Those Europeans and Americans who engaged in illegal slave trading did so in order to avoid paying taxes on the slaves that they carried. Others traded without receiving permission to do so from the authorities or began smuggling slaves after laws were passed abolishing the human traffic. In spite of these difficulties, most historians now estimate that the number of Africans who arrived as slaves from 1502 to the mid 19th century amounted to between 10 and 12 million. Most of these people were shipped to Latin America and the Caribbean.

The foundations of the Atlantic slave trade were established in the 16th century by Spanish colonists, who were no strangers to the institution of slavery. Prior to Columbus's voyages to the Americas, the Spaniards held Muslims, black Africans, Slavs, and even other Spaniards as slaves. In fact, the number of African slaves in Spain and Portugal was increasing during the years preceding Columbus's voyages, reflecting a decline in the use of other groups as slaves.

Under the circumstances, it is not surprising that the Spaniards in Hispaniola, the first colony in the Caribbean, asked the Crown to send them African slaves once the need for labor arose. This request was

An African slave waits on a wealthy Portuguese family. In the years before Columbus's voyages, the number of Africans enslaved in Spain and Portugal increased.

made in 1501, a mere seven years after the island had been colonized. Unwilling to perform menial and back-breaking tasks, the Spaniards had expected to depend on the forced labor of the native peoples. The Indians, at least those who fell under the control of the colonists, were enslaved and required to work in the fields, households, and mines. But many Indians soon died from mistreatment and disease, which created a shortage of labor.

Faced with a declining supply of Indian laborers, the Spanish colonists had to ponder their options. They could have decided to do all the work themselves. But this alternative was never seriously considered. The colonists could have abandoned the colonial enterprise and returned home. There is no evidence that this option was ever entertained. Finally, they could have made arrangements to import other Spaniards to do the work, much the same way that the English colonists would do a century later in North America. Under what was known as the indentured labor system, the English colonists paid the passage of an assortment of people—farmers, laborers, servant, artisans, convicts, and the unemployed—who were interested in immigrating to North America. In return, these individuals signed an indenture, or contract, to work for the person who paid the passage, usually for a period of four to seven years.

Rejecting, or at least not considering, these options, the Spanish colonists decided to introduce African slavery. Not only were Africans performing unpaid labor in Spain and elsewhere in Europe at the time, but as a group they were placed at the bottom of the social order as well. The terms "black" and "slave" had become increasingly interchangeable in Spain in the 15th century. The country's moral climate justified African slavery. In other words, black Africans had occupied a decidedly inferior place in Spanish society prior to Columbus's expeditions. In addition, the notion that Africans could be enslaved and were suited for that condition had become widely accepted and deeply rooted in Spanish society.

It is not entirely clear why this was the case. Spaniards, and by extension the Portuguese and other Europeans, may have attributed negative qualities to the Africans because they were different culturally, had black skins, and were not Christians. Africans were people set apart as the "other," persons whose differences the Europeans neither appreciated, respected, nor understood. Not until the 19th century, however, did a full-blown racist ideology, or system of beliefs, develop to promote the biological claims to superiority by whites and to defend the treatment of blacks by alleging that they were inferior members of the human species. No such "scientific" claims were made at the time of Columbus. Perhaps none was needed. By purchasing Africans and using them as slaves, the Europeans were already asserting power over them. In time, the Africans' inferior place in society came to be seen as normal, and few voices were raised to challenge their treatment and condition.

In response to the request from the governor of Hispaniola for African slave labor in 1501, the Spanish Crown authorized the shipment of slaves in 1502. The slaves in this first cargo had lived in Spain for some time before they were shipped to the Caribbean. Not until 1518 would slaves be transported to the Americas directly from Africa.

The Portuguese were the pioneering European slave traders. Portugal was the first country in Europe that had developed the technology to conduct a seafaring trade. Unlike some of the other European countries, Portugal was politically united by the 15th century and free from the sorts of serious internal conflicts that weakened its neighbors. As a result, its leaders could focus their energies on overseas expansion and trade. Situated on the Atlantic Ocean, the Portuguese had also made significant advances in shipbuilding, thereby giving them the ability to participate actively in overseas trading ventures. Portugal had also developed a class of merchants and entrepreneurs with the wealth, skill, and experience to conduct a slave trade. The traders were men with an adventurous spirit, a "thirst for riches," as one observer described them at the time, and a curiosity to explore other societies.

Prince Henry, who would later be called "the Navigator," was one of the earliest of the Portuguese explorers. His explorations along the African coast in the 1420s opened the way for the development of a European-African trade in black slaves. The first organized Portuguese expedition to capture black Africans and enslave them appears to have occurred in 1441. Led by Antão Gonçalves and Nuno Tristão, the members of the expedition captured 12 Africans off the coast of northern Mauritania and presented them at the Portuguese court.

This initial Portuguese success at people-stealing encouraged additional attempts. A few kidnapped Africans were brought to Portugal in succeeding months, but the single largest group was unloaded in Lisbon

A carved ivory salt-cellar by an African artist depicts Portuguese slave traders. The Portuguese began exploring the coast of Africa in the 1420s, and they made their first expedition to capture Africans as slaves in 1441.

on August 8, 1444. There were between 235 and 240 captives in this party. In time, Genoese, Florentine, and Castilian traders joined the Portuguese kidnappers on the West African coast. But the Portuguese remained the principal carriers of Africans to Europe for the next century and more. The process by which these Africans were acquired in the early years cannot be characterized as a trade. The evidence does not show that the Europeans bargained with anyone; the Africans were simply abducted. Portuguese authorities, however, imposed a tax on all Africans sold in their country.

Not surprisingly, the Europeans could not continue to kidnap Africans indefinitely, and a trade with its own rules would have to be developed. To this end, the Portuguese built a fort on the island of Arguin to serve as a base for trade with the Africans. This did not mean that raids for African slaves ceased; it indicated that the contact with Africa was being placed on a more formal footing and that the abductions decreased even if they did not disappear. By 1450 the Portuguese had begun to transport an average of 1,000 to 2,000 African slaves to Europe each year. Most of these people came from the Senegambia, but a few were from other nearby areas.

Portugal's domination of the Euro-African trade deepened as the 15th century wore on. In 1452, Pope Nicholas V granted the Portuguese king the authority to attack and enslave "the Moors, heathens and other enemies of Christ" who lived south of Cape Bojador. Although this and other papal grants did not necessarily lead to an increase in the number of slaves, they gave the approval of the church to the institution of slavery and paved the way for Portuguese conquest and occupation of societies that were not Christian. In 1479, Spain recognized Portugal's supremacy in the slave trade by signing the Treaty of Aláçovas. The treaty granted Portugal the right to supply Spain with African slaves and accepted its monopoly, or total control, of the African trade. Three years later, in 1482, the Portuguese built a fort on the Gold Coast (modern Ghana) to encourage, assist, and protect the expanding African commerce. Known as Elmina Castle, the fort could hold hundreds of slaves.

Clearly, when the Spanish Crown agreed to send African slaves to Hispaniola in 1502, the bureaucratic machinery of treaties and established practices was already in place to acquire them. Under the terms of the 1479 treaty, the Portuguese had already agreed to supply African slaves to the Spaniards. So the decline of the Indian population of the Americas and the Spanish colonists' insistence on a new labor force did not create the African slave trade and slavery. Both were already in existence. The demand for slaves in the Americas, did, however, lead to an

expansion of the trade and a change in its direction. Instead of going up to Europe, the majority of the Africans would soon be sent across the Atlantic to the Americas.

The increase in the demand for slaves, coupled with the expectation that huge profits could be made, led several other European nations to participate in the slave trade. By 1650, the Dutch, the English, and the French, among others, had joined the Portuguese in this human commerce. Spain, whose colonies consumed most of the African slaves during the first century and a half of the slave trade, did no trading on the African coast until the late 18th century. This was not by design. It was a consequence of another treaty signed by Spain and Portugal in 1494. Known as the Treaty of Tordesillas, the agreement permitted the Portuguese to trade on the African coast and in Asia and Brazil. The Spaniards were confined to the rest of what became known as the

The Portuguese built Elmina Castle in 1482 as a base for the slave trade. The fort could hold hundreds of slaves.

28

Americas. The other European nations, however, were not parties to this division of the known world. They did not feel themselves bound by the treaty, and they ignored it.

Once the Spanish Crown authorized the introduction of African slaves in the Americas, it issued licenses to individual traders to supply the slaves. These traders were likely to be either Portuguese, Genoese, or Spaniards. In return for a license, the traders had to pay a fee. The license specified the number of slaves that would be delivered and the destination. A new license was required for each slave-trading journey because the Crown wanted to exercise control over the supply of slaves and to receive the tax revenue that the trade generated. Most traders received permission to deliver fewer than 20 or 30 slaves. There were exceptions, of course, and some traders were allowed to ship hundreds of slaves at one time. Spaniards who intended to settle in the colonies were also allowed to take with them any slaves that they already owned.

The system of awarding licenses did not satisfy the growing demand for unfree African labor. Some traders did not fulfill their contractual

This drawing shows the layout of a European slave-trading center in West Africa. By the mid-17th century, Portugal, England, France, Holland, and other European countries were involved in the trade of African slaves.

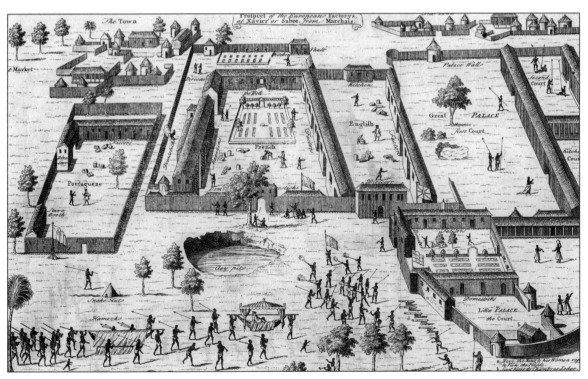

obligations for one reason or another. Slave deliveries were often delayed, and Africans never arrived in adequate numbers to meet the demand.

In spite of the bureaucratic and other problems that the licensing system produced, it was not replaced until 1595. In that year, the Spanish Crown introduced a monopoly system known as the *Asiento,* or *contract.* Under this system, a trader or a trading company was granted the sole right to supply a given number of slaves, usually several thousand each year, to the colonies for a specified number of years. These contracts were awarded only after the Crown received bids from prospective traders. The traders who were chosen had to pay a sizeable fee when they received the contract.

Most, if not all, of these traders failed to meet the terms of their agreements. Some ran into financial difficulties, and others were more interested in engaging in other forms of commerce, such as trading in silver and other precious metals or in textiles. The failure of the *Asentistas* to meet their contractual obligations paved the way for other traders to smuggle slaves into the colonies. The smugglers were likely to be Portuguese, Spanish, Dutch, or English traders.

The business of the Atlantic slave trade was helped by the existence of slavery and a slave trade inside Africa. As was the case with various societies in Asia, Europe, and the Americas, forms of servitude existed among African ethnic groups. Captives taken in war, debtors, and persons convicted of certain crimes, such as homicides, could lose their liberty. These people still had some rights, however. They could marry, inherit property, and participate extensively in the life of the host society. Over time, most slaves could expect to receive their freedom. The pace at which this occurred must have varied, but the expectation that freedom was within reach probably made their condition more endurable.

Still, the Atlantic slave trade did not develop *because* slavery already existed in Africa. Such a claim would place the primary responsibility for the human traffic on the shoulders of the African peoples. The European and American traders joined hands with their African counterparts to conduct a mutually beneficial commerce. It was a trade like any other, bound by the rules of supply and demand, profit and loss. But the slave trade differed from other forms of business in one important respect: the trading goods were other human beings. It is this crucial difference that explains the horror of the slave trade and the moral revulsion that it would later produce.

The rules governing the slave trade took their distinctive shape during the second half of the 15th century. Once the external demand for African workers began to increase, the process by which they were acquired fell under the control of the local traders. Although European traders continued to abduct unsuspecting Africans, the number of such raids diminished. The African leaders and their peoples had to assert control over what was taking place in their territory and could not allow foreigners to kidnap their citizens at will. Such atrocities undermined the stability of the society and constituted an assault on the people. The African rulers also realized that if the developing trade were organized and regulated, they could make money from it. Among other things, a tax was imposed on the sale of each slave.

Portuguese traders obtained their slave cargoes for the Americas from West Africa as well as from the Congo and Angola, which are located in West Central Africa. Until about 1600, the majority of the slaves came from West Africa, from a vast area north of the equator. This region includes modern Senegal, Gambia, Guinea-Bissau, and Sierra Leone. The ethnic groups that made up these slave cargoes included the Wolof and the Serer from Senegal; the Mandinka from the Gambia; the Bram, Banyun, and Biafada from Guinea-Bissau. The Baga, Temne, and Landuma peoples came from Sierra Leone. The Congo-Angola region provided the Bakongo, Teke, and Ambundu peoples. Probably about one-third of the slaves originated in the Congo-Angola region, and about 25 percent each came from the Senegambia and Guinea-Bissau.

The sources for the supply of slaves kept shifting throughout the entire history of the African slave trade. Much depended on political developments in the various societies. Whenever states were at war, and if these wars continued for long periods of time, the captives would be made available for sale to European traders. Such was the case of the states in the Senegambia in the 16th century and of the kingdom of Kongo during the same period. Angola increasingly became the chief source of slaves as the 16th century progressed. This was the result of the political disorder that wracked the various states in the area. By 1600, slave cargoes also included the Akan from the Gold Coast (modern

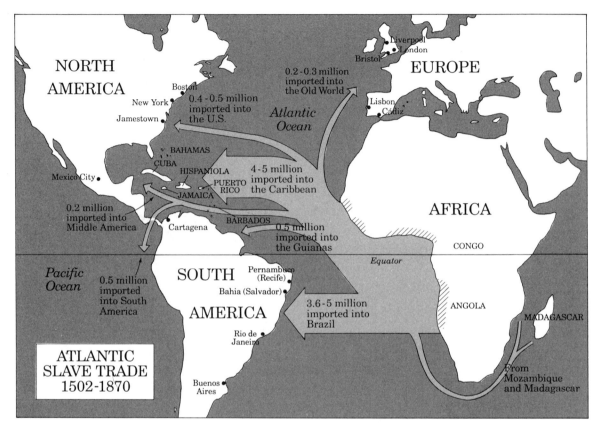

ATLANTIC SLAVE TRADE 1502-1870

Ghana), the Fon from coastal Dahomey, and the Ibo from eastern Nigeria. A few persons also came from southeastern Africa, principally from Mozambique. Overall, West Central Africa supplied about 40 percent of the slaves between the 16th and 19th centuries.

The political divisions among the African peoples largely account for the availability of slaves for the Atlantic market. Africa has never been a politically united continent whose peoples had a common identity and consciousness—either during the 16th century, or at any time during the course of the slave trade, or later. Hardly anyone would have described himself or herself as an "African." Residents of the continent were more likely to think of themselves as belonging to specific ethnic groups, such as the Ibo, Biafada, Bram, or Mandinka. The concept of an African identity above and beyond ethnic and geographic boundaries is a relatively recent development.

West and West Central Africa, from which most of the captives

This map shows where African slaves were shipped during the Atlantic slave trade. Between 10 and 12 million African slaves were imported into the Americas.

were taken, consisted of a large number of states. Some of these were relatively small, while others, such as the kingdom of Kongo and the Jolof Empire in the Senegambia, were very large and included various mini-states that they had absorbed. These states frequently had disputes that led to warfare. In some cases, larger and more powerful states attempted to overrun their smaller neighbors. These instances of territorial expansion often led to prolonged conflicts and the taking of prisoners. Other conflicts between states arose from commercial rivalries, struggles to control trade routes, and even efforts to determine who would succeed to the leadership of bordering states. The political fragmentation of the different regions, coupled with the varieties of conflicts that led to war, created a constant flow of human victims for the trade.

The vast majority of the slaves were prisoners of war. The seller and the victim usually belonged to different states and were enemies. Accordingly, Africans did not "sell their own people," as some historians have maintained. Such a claim ignores the culturally and politically diverse nature of the regions from which the slaves came as well as the

A boatload of African slaves is delivered to a Portuguese ship bound for the Americas. Most African slaves were prisoners of war who were sold to European traders by Africans.

33

A slave trader brands an African slave with the mark of the slave's buyer. Slaves were branded so escapees could be easily identified and returned to their owners.

diversity of the African continent as a whole. The overwhelming majority—perhaps 80 percent—of the victims of the human traffic were likely to be persons who had no ties to the state of their sellers, had no rights, and were vulnerable to the traditional fate of wartime prisoners—imprisonment, enslavement, or death.

There were undoubtedly instances of individuals who were kidnapped by unscrupulous fellow citizens and sold. Such atrocities invited severe punishment. No society, of course, could survive for long if individuals were allowed to seize and sell others at will. As William Bosman, an 18th-century Dutch trader, wrote: "Not a few in our country fondly imagine that parents here [Africa] sell their children, men their wives and one brother the other, but those who think so deceive themselves."

Little is known about the process by which the slaves were traded during the early years. (Information is much more readily available for the years after 1650.) Still, it is known that the European traders exchanged textile products, guns, gunpowder, alcohol, pots and pans, and a range of other consumer goods for the slaves. The value of each slave was arrived at after much bargaining between the black and the white traders. The process evidently became more complicated in the 17th century, when more Europeans entered the trade, bringing a wider variety of products with values expressed in their own currency. Thus, in addition to the Portuguese escudo, the Africans had to get accustomed to the English pound sterling, the Dutch guilder, and the French franc. The Africans, too, had different monetary systems. There was the iron bar in Sierra Leone, gold in Ghana, cowrie shells in Dahomey, and Loango cloth in Angola.

Once the African was sold, he or she was usually branded with the identification mark of the purchaser. Whether this was a regular practice in the early years is uncertain, but it would become so in the 17th century and later. A slave who was branded could be identified in the event of escape or if the individual were stolen by a European competitor. There was, understandably, not much honor in the slave-trading business.

The slaves' journey to the coast and to the waiting ships could be quite hazardous. Prodded by their captors, some perished along the way as a consequence of disease and wounds infected by branding. Death was an ever-present feature of the trade. Many more would die as they awaited departure on the coast for the Americas, and others would succumb during the Atlantic crossing.

An African trader marches a group of prisoners to a waiting ship, where they will be sold as slaves. The journey to trading centers exposed captives to physical abuse, exhaustion, and disease, and many died before being sold into slavery.

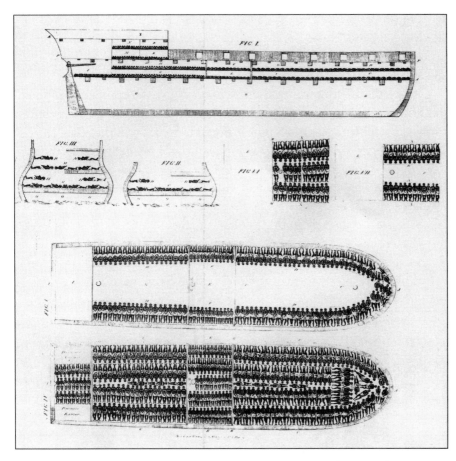

This illustration shows how African slaves were jammed onto ships bound for the Americas. Many slaves died during the journey from Africa to the Americas, which was known as the middle passage.

The length of time that the human cargoes waited in the forts on the coast prior to their departure for the Americas varied. Much depended on the supply of slaves to be purchased. This, in turn, was related to whether the states were at war, which would generate captives who could be sold. Once the traders had acquired their full cargo, the long and terrible journey to the Americas began.

The journey from Africa to the Americas was known as the middle passage. It derived its name from the second, or middle, segment of a European-based slave ship's triangular route. The first leg was the trip from Europe to Africa, and the third was the ship's return journey from the Americas to Europe. The middle passage, however, remains the most horrible symbol of the traffic in human beings. Chained together and confined to the cramped, hot, and humid holds of the ships, these

Slaves were chained together and squeezed into the holds of ships. The blacks transported to the Americas this way suffered the ravages of hunger, thirst, disease, and brutality.

Africans were lucky if they survived the ordeal. The sanitary conditions aboard these slave ships were appalling, producing the perfect environment for the spread of disease. Some slaves were already ill before they embarked, and others were tormented by disease on board the ship. Dysentery, measles, smallpox, yellow fever, dehydration, and a variety of "fevers" proved to be the scourge of every journey.

It was, of course, impossible to predict how many slaves would die during the crossing. The *Asiento* contracts that the Spaniards awarded usually made allowances for a death rate of between 10 percent and 40 percent on each cargo. But it is not entirely clear whether this was an accurate estimate for the 16th century. Friar Tomás de Mercado, who lived in Mexico in the 1580s, maintained that the death rate at the time was less than 20 percent. Such an estimate, however, should be viewed with caution. Mercado commented on the conditions aboard the ships:

> They embark four to five hundred of them in a boat which sometimes is not a cargo boat. The very stench is enough to kill most of them, and indeed many of them die. The wonder is that twenty percent of them are not lost. Of five-hundred taken from Cape Verde to New Spain [Mexico] in one vessel one hundred and twenty died in one night because they packed them like pigs or worse, all below decks, where their very breath and excrement (which are sufficient to pollute any atmosphere and destroy them all) killed them. The crew also died. The sad affair does not end there, for before they reached Mexico, almost three hundred had died.

The death rate not only reflected the sanitary conditions aboard the ships, but it was also related to the general health of the slaves before the journey began. Chance, or luck, played a part as well. If there was no one

37

on board who carried an infectious disease, such as smallpox, the cargo would most likely experience a lower than average death rate.

There was also a relationship between the time the ship took to cross the Atlantic and the death toll. The faster the sailing time, the lower the death rate. During the 16th century it took anywhere from 12 to 20 weeks to reach the American ports. Such a long confinement at sea in close quarters aided the spread of disease. With the construction of faster ships in the 18th and 19th centuries, the sailing time ranged between five and eight weeks. The average death rate in the 18th century was between 10 percent and 15 percent; by the 19th century it had fallen to somewhere between 5 percent and 10 percent. Sanitary conditions had improved aboard the ships, and better medical care was provided.

Thoughtful captains took care to provide their human cargoes with a diet consisting of the foods to which they were accustomed. The composition of these foods varied, depending on the part of Africa from which the slaves came. In general, however, such foods included corn, yams, palm oil, rice, and potatoes. Slave ships also stocked foodstuffs that they brought from Europe, such as bread, cheese, beef, beans, and flour. However, these supplies sometimes proved inadequate to feed a cargo of slaves, particularly if the journey to the Americas lasted longer than had been expected. Reports from the 18th century and later described voyages that ran out of food and slaves who arrived thin and hungry.

The slaves must have engaged in forms of resistance on board ships during this early period, but the surviving records shed no light on this issue. Ships did, however, carry a variety of gadgets—such as mouth openers, thumb screws, chains, and whips—to punish those who resisted their condition. During the 18th and 19th centuries slaves participated in rebellions and hunger strikes, jumped overboard, and verbally abused the crew. Such physical challenges to slavery on the high seas were seldom successful, but they often resulted in considerable loss of life.

The arrival of the slaves in such places as Hispaniola, Lima, and Vera Cruz signaled the end of one awful experience and the beginning of another. The Africans were purchased yet again and became the property of strange people in a strange land. Their prospects of returning to their homeland were virtually nonexistent. Their ties with their kith and kin were severed forever, and their sense of alienation in their new lands must have been paralyzing. There are no firsthand accounts, however, of

Authorities capture a ship attempting to smuggle slaves into Cuba without a license. The slaves would have been returned to West Africa and set free.

the reactions of the Africans upon their arrival in the Americas in the early years. But we do have a particularly poignant description of the emotions of that first large slave cargo that disembarked in Lisbon in 1444. The Portuguese chronicler, Eannes Zurara, was moved to write:

> But what heart could be so hard as not to be pierced with piteous feeling to see that company? For some kept their heads low and their faces bathed in tears, looking one upon another; others stood groaning very dolorously, looking up to the height of heaven, fixing their eyes upon it, crying out loudly, as if asking help of the Father of Nature; others struck their faces with the palms of their hands, throwing themselves at full length upon the ground; others made their lamentations in the manner of a dirge, after the custom of their country. And though we could not understand the words of their language, the sound of it right well accorded with the measure of their sadness. But to increase their sufferings still more, there now arrived those who had charge of the division of the captives, and who began to separate

one from another, in order to make an equal partition of the fifths; and then was it needful to part fathers from sons, husbands from wives, brothers from brothers. No respect was shewn either to friends or relations, but each fell where his lot took him. . . . And who could finish that partition without very great toil? For as often as they placed them in one part the sons, seeing their fathers in another, rose with great energy and rushed over to them; the mothers clasped their other children in their arms, and threw themselves flat on the ground with them, receiving blows with little pity for their own flesh, if only they might not be torn from them.

Where did the slaves who arrived in the Americas go? The vast majority, approximately 95 percent, were distributed to the societies of Latin America and the Caribbean. Only about 5 percent ended up in the British colonies of North America, or what is now the United States. The following figures are a reasonably accurate accounting of the distribution patterns of the trade based upon present knowledge:

British North America	550,000
Spanish America	2,000,000
British Caribbean	2,500,000 to 3,000,000
French Caribbean	1,600,000
Dutch Caribbean	50,000
Brazil	4,000,000 to 5,000,000
Danish Caribbean	50,000

Almost all of the slaveholding societies of the Americas experienced an annual decrease in population as the Africans fell victim to hard work and disease. As a result, they had to depend on the slave trade to replenish their labor supply. The only exception to this pattern was English North America. By the first decades of the 18th century, the North American slave population began to reproduce itself, and it sustained this growth until emancipation came in the 1860s. For this reason, North America was much less dependent on the slave trade than the other slave societies of the Americas, which had a profound influence on the culture of the black population in this region. The North American slave population by the 19th century was essentially a creole, or locally born, population. Although only about 500,000 Africans had been imported into that society, the slave population numbered almost 4 million in 1860, just before the outbreak of the Civil War.

The African slave trade to the Americas lasted for more than three and a half centuries. Perhaps as many as 300,000 enslaved people arrived during the first century of its existence, but the 18th century represented the most active years of the trade. Regardless of the century in which they arrived, however, these human beings had to confront the challenge of making a new life for themselves in new lands under the most difficult circumstances.

CHAPTER 2
THE WORLDS OF SLAVERY AND WORK

African slaves were first brought to the Americas in the 16th century to meet the economic needs of Spanish and Portuguese colonists. The first slaves arrived in Hispaniola in 1502; thousands more would experience a similar fate as the century progressed. From Hispaniola the institution of slavery spread to the other islands in the Caribbean that were colonized by the Spaniards—Puerto Rico, Cuba, and Jamaica. Eventually, such mainland colonies as Mexico, Peru, Venezuela, Bolivia, and those in Central America became the new homes of thousands of unfree African workers. Brazil, a Portuguese colony, was no exception; by 1600 it joined Mexico and Peru as one of the three largest slave-holding societies.

The Spaniards and the Portuguese were not the only slaveholders in the Americas. In time, African slaves were used in all of the European colonies. By 1650, for example, the English had begun to use enslaved Africans in their Caribbean and North American colonies. The Dutch, the French, and the Danes would soon do likewise. So great was the demand for African labor that an average of 60,000 slaves were imported annually during the 18th century.

Of the 300,000 Africans who arrived before 1620, the greatest number, probably around 80,000, went to Mexico. This colony received most

Slaves mine and wash gold as a Spanish overseer counts the nuggets. African slaves in the Americas performed a variety of tasks, from laboring in mines and on plantations to building houses and doing household work.

UNITED STATES OF AMERICA

*Atlantic
Ocean*

MEXICO

BAHAMAS

*Tropic of
Cancer*

Mexico
City ●

Veracruz

CUBA

DOMINICAN REPUBLIC

PUERTO RICO

Acapulco ●

BELIZE

JAMAICA

HAITI

GUATEMALA
EL SALVADOR
HONDURAS
NICARAGUA
COSTA RICA
PANAMA

BARBADOS
TRINIDAD AND TOBAGO
GUYANA
SURINAME
FRENCH GUIANA

VENEZUELA

Bogotá
COLOMBIA

Equator

Galapagos Islands
(Ecuador)

ECUADOR

PERU

● Lima

*Pacific
Ocean*

BRAZIL

BOLIVIA

Rio de
Janeiro

*Tropic of
Capricorn*

PARAGUAY

São Paulo

ARGENTINA

URUGUAY

CHILE

Buenos
Aires

THE AMERICAS

*African slaves were
imported into all
parts of the
Caribbean and
throughout North
and South America.*

of its slaves after 1570, when the Indian population began a rapid decline. Once the local population began to recover in the mid 17th
century and a racially mixed group emerged (mestizos, the children of
Spaniards and Indians), fewer Africans were imported. The other

mainland colonies and the Caribbean islands received another 80,000 to 90,000 slaves before 1620. Portuguese Brazil did not begin to import Africans until the mid 16th century, but it received an ever-increasing number throughout the rest of that century and in succeeding years. By 1620 that colony had imported an estimated 130,000 slaves.

Regardless of where the slaves went, the colonial authorities introduced laws that defined their status and regulated their behavior. Because the Spaniards and the Portuguese owned slaves before they came to the Americas, they had already developed rules governing their behavior, rights, and treatment. The Spanish slave laws were a part of a larger body of laws and moral principles that formed the basis of the Spanish legal system. Known as *Las Siete Partidas* (the Seven Parts), these laws granted slaves the right to marry, inherit property, and to be freed under certain conditions. The *Partidas* imposed limits on the masters' ability to mistreat their slaves, and slaves could appeal to the local authorities if their rights were violated. It is not known whether the law was always enforced.

The situation in Portugal, at least in theory, was somewhat different. At the time when Brazil was colonized in the 16th century, the mother country did not have a body of laws similar to the *Siete Partidas*. Rather, each town had its own rules, and there does not appear to have been much uniformity in content or enforcement. Accordingly, the Crown filled the breach by issuing appropriate laws when the need arose. The English, French, and Dutch had no preexisting law of slavery. As a result, these nations developed their colonial slave laws in a piecemeal fashion, as the need arose.

The slave laws that the Spanish colonists introduced in the 16th century in Hispaniola, Mexico, Peru, and elsewhere shared many features. In general, these laws were much harsher than those existing in Spain. Outnumbered by a servile population of Indians and Africans in the 16th century, the colonists tried to impose rigid controls over those whom they exploited and enslaved. Essentially, the laws were designed to protect the slaveholding class from the angry reprisals of their human property.

The earliest legislation concerning black slaves that the colonial governments introduced prohibited them from owning or carrying weapons. In Mexico, for example, such laws were placed on the books at

various times beginning in 1537. Peru issued its first series of restrictive measures in 1545 and repeated the measures in succeeding years to ensure enforcement. Such restrictive legislation also established the punishment for assaulting whites. According to a 1552 law, slaves who took up arms against a Spaniard in Mexico were liable to receive 100 lashes in addition to having a nail driven through their hands. Slaves would have their hands cut off if they repeated the offense.

As the slave populations increased, colonial authorities imposed a series of controls on almost every aspect of the Africans' public lives. Although the details varied, slaves were forbidden to be out of doors after dark, and could not travel freely or gather in large groups except for religious purposes. Insecure masters wanted to take no chances; they had to ensure that their human property lacked the opportunity or the means to launch movements to claim their freedom. But such restrictions did not always have the desired results.

Although the slave owners and other whites feared black slaves, colonial society increasingly became dependent on them for a variety of services. As soon as blacks began to arrive in the colonies, the Spaniards used them to help subjugate the native peoples and to explore for new territories to seize. Hernan Cortés, who defeated the Aztecs, is said to

A black soldier accompanies a Spanish officer as he confronts the indigenous peoples of Mexico. The Spaniards used African slaves to help them conquer the native peoples and to explore new territories in the Americas to claim for the Spanish Crown.

have had 300 African slaves with him in Mexico in 1522. African slaves accompanied the Spaniards on their various military invasions of Peru beginning in 1524. A number of them participated in explorations into Chile and other areas on the coast and in the interior. A black man was among the four Spanish soldiers chosen by the Spanish conquistador Francisco Pizarro to be in the advance party to survey the Inca capital at Cuzco, Peru. Slaves also participated in the Spanish military expeditions against the Indians in Honduras in the 1550s.

Perhaps the best-known African-born explorer of the Americas in the 16th century was a man known historically as Esteban or Estevanico. He was born in Morocco in the early 16th century and ended up as a slave in Spain. In 1528 Esteban was a member of an expedition that left Spain with the objective of seizing Florida from the native inhabitants. The expedition fell on hard times, and most of the explorers died. Esteban survived and, along with three other men, started an extraordinary odyssey that took him through Texas and eventually ended in Mexico City. The journey lasted eight years. In 1539 he took part in

African slaves, depicted here with European features, work inside a sugar mill in Hispaniola. African slaves were usually assigned to do the most strenuous work in the colonies.

another expedition to the northern frontiers of Mexico, leading the group that first encountered the Zuni Indians and reached what is now New Mexico. The intrepid explorer was killed by the Indians soon after he met them.

Although blacks aided the Spaniards in their military expeditions, such roles paled in comparison to their sustained importance as workers. As soon as they began to arrive in Hispaniola in 1502, slaves assumed the most strenuous tasks, setting a precedent for other slaveholding societies. The colonists in these early years were particularly interested in mining for precious metals and constantly appealed for black slaves. The Crown was willing to agree because it received a one-fifth share of the proceeds of the mines. In 1505, for example, King Ferdinand informed the governor of Hispaniola that "I will send more Negro slaves as you request. I think there may be a hundred. At each time a trustworthy person will go with them who may share in the gold they may collect." So important would Africans become as workers in the Americas that one official in Mexico reported in 1537 that "I have written to Spain for black slaves because I consider them indispensable for the cultivation of the land and the increase of royal revenue."

Without a doubt, black slaves played the most important roles in the mining industry during the 16th century. Mining was a particularly hazardous activity, and the death rate of those involved in it tended to be quite high. The Indian workers died quickly, and the Spaniards as a group did not find the occupation attractive. African slaves were imported as substitutes, and they, too, suffered a high death rate. In 1511, King Ferdinand lamented in a letter to the authorities in Hispaniola, "I do not understand how so many negroes have died; take much care of them."

The Africans were used first in the copper and gold mines of Hispaniola, but these metals were not abundant there. The industry soon collapsed. On the other hand, the mainland colonies of Mexico and Peru were extremely rich in silver deposits. By 1550 the colonists had found silver in northern Mexico at Zacatecas, Guanajuato, and Pachuca. Deposits of silver were also uncovered at Michoacan, Tasco, Temascaltepec, and other places. In Peru, silver veins were struck in the highland areas of Potosí and Porco, and rich gold deposits were discovered at Chachapoyas and Carabaya.

Workers toil in a silver mine in Peru. When the native peoples in some societies died off because of disease, warfare, and the rigors and hazardous conditions in the mines, European colonists imported African slaves as an alternative labor force.

Shortly after the discovery of the first silver veins in Mexico, Viceroy Antonio de Mendoza requested that the authorities in Spain send Africans because "the silver mines are increasing, as each day more and more are discovered while the [Indian] slaves continue to decrease." A sympathetic Crown responded favorably to these pleas, but the supply of Africans could not keep abreast of the demand for them in the mines and other economic enterprises. The high death rate of the Africans and Indians employed in the mining industry from accidents (such as collapsing underground roofs) and lung diseases also made the labor problem more severe.

Some of those who advocated the importation of Africans wanted to relieve the Indians of the burdensome labor of the mines. Another Mexican viceroy, the Marques de Villamanrique, was one such person. In 1586, for example, he noted the "dangerous" and "excessive" nature of the work in which the Indians were engaged in the mines. In order to protect them from such exploitation he asked that 3,000 or 4,000 Africans be sent. Four years later, in an attempt to increase the servile labor force, the viceroy recommended that all free blacks and mulattoes (children of Spaniards and blacks) in the colony be forced to labor in the mines. Not only would they serve as a substitute for Indian workers, the viceroy reasoned, but they would also earn wages and "their children growing up in that life would become fond of it."

Black slaves also played critically important roles in the textile factories of Mexico and, to a lesser extent, Peru. These workshops, known as *obrajes,* manufactured cloth for the residents of the colonies. The workers in these factories were often physically abused and forced to labor for long hours in cramped, hot, and humid quarters. The Crown was concerned about the poor working conditions in these hell houses and wanted to protect the Indians in Mexico from being employed in them. In 1601 the Crown prohibited Indian workers from laboring in the Mexican *obrajes* and repeated the ban in 1609, probably because it was not being enforced. In both instances, the Crown decreed that black slaves should replace the Indians. Clearly, the Crown saw black workers as suited for the most difficult tasks in society and seemed unconcerned about the inhumane conditions under which they worked. There was nothing particularly new about this attitude; black workers in Spain had experienced a similar fate.

As soon as it became clear that the early mining economy in the islands would collapse because of the depletion of the mineral resources, the Spanish colonists embraced other pursuits. The climate and soil of the Caribbean proved ideal for sugarcane cultivation, and in 1506 the colonists in Hispaniola began to experiment with growing that crop. The Spaniards and the Portuguese had been familiar with sugarcane cultivation for centuries before the Columbus voyages. By the mid 15th century, the Portuguese had begun to use African slaves on their sugar-

An African slave cuts down sugarcane in the Caribbean.

cane plantations in the Atlantic islands of Madeira, São Tomé, the Azores, the Canaries, and Cape Verde. Africans who were experienced in the techniques of sugarcane cultivation and the sugar industry must have comprised some of the slave cargoes to the Americas.

The first sugar mill (*ingenio*) in the Caribbean was constructed in Hispaniola in 1516, and by 1548 the island had 35 of them, the most that would exist there at any one time in the 16th century. Sugarcane cultivation also spread to the other islands of Puerto Rico, Jamaica, and Cuba. Although Hispaniola began to export sugar in 1521, the sugar industry did not flourish anywhere in the Caribbean in the 16th century. Not until after 1650 did sugar become "king" in the islands, particularly in the English, Dutch, and French colonies.

Sugarcane cultivation, aided by the extensive use of African slave labor, underwent its greatest expansion on the mainland during the 16th century. Mexico and Brazil became particularly important as sugar-producing colonies, but cane was also cultivated in Peru, Venezuela, and elsewhere. Because the Portuguese dominated the slave trade, Brazil received an ever-expanding supply of African labor. By 1580, this colony not only boasted a large black population but was the principal supplier of sugar to European markets.

Mexico was the earliest of the mainland colonies to grow sugarcane. Because of their agreeable climates, the tropical areas surrounding Vera Cruz and the warm valleys of Michoacan, Huatusco, Córdoba, and Oaxaca quickly became major centers of sugarcane cultivation. Historians are not certain when the colonists first started to grow the cane; contemporary sources indicate that it began between 1524 and 1530. African slaves seemed to have been used in the industry from the outset.

Sugarcane plantations in 16th-century Mexico were of various sizes, depending on the availability of capital, land, and labor. There were some extremely large ones by the last decades of the 16th century, employing scores of African workers. In 1580, a plantation at Orizaba reported the presence of 123 African slaves, and in 1606 the Santísima Trinidad plantation in Jalapa had 200. Most plantations probably employed fewer Africans, and almost all appear to have had Indian workers as well.

The Crown did not take kindly to the use of Indians on the sugar plantations. The work was demanding, and it was believed that the native

The SUGAR-CANE, SUGAR-MILL, &c.

peoples lacked the physical strength to do the work. In fact, Spanish colonists on the mainland and in the Caribbean islands believed that one African could do the work of four Indians. This kind of mythology ensured that blacks would not only be in great demand but would be assigned the most strenuous tasks. As early as 1542, the Crown prohibited the use of Indian workers in the more demanding jobs on the plantations "because one plantation is sufficient to kill two thousand of them each year." Forty-two years later, the Mexican viceroy observed that the Indians who worked in the *ingenio* at Orizaba "experience notable pressures and problems" because they "are used in the boiling house and at difficult and more intolerable tasks that are most suited to Negro slaves accustomed to performing such difficult jobs and [who are] not weak and frail Indians with little strength and stamina."

Work on the sugar plantations in Mexico and elsewhere extracted a heavy toll from the Africans. The hours were long—up to 20 per day at harvest time. At the Xochimaneas hacienda in southern Mexico, owned by the Society of Jesus,

> slaves were generally awakened at four in the morning and worked until ten or eleven o'clock at night. Upon arising, the slaves went to the sugar mill where they ground eight, nine, or ten caldrons of sugar "depending on the cane and the season." At daybreak the sound of a bell summoned the slaves

An overseer directs slaves at a sugar mill in the 17th century. Sugarcane cultivation was introduced to the Caribbean shortly after the establishment of Spanish colonial rule. It eventually became an important industry there.

to take the sugar from the boiling house (casa de calderas) to the refinery (casa de purgar) and to put the "white sugar" in the sun to be dried. When there was no sugar to be sunned, the slaves occupied themselves with other tasks. When this work was completed, they returned to their homes for breakfast and to ready themselves for the fields.

Accidents occurred in the *ingenios* and the overall death rate in the sugar plantations seemed to have been as high as that in the mines, if not higher. The Mexican viceroy confessed in 1599 that African slaves who worked in the sugar industry had a death rate in excess of "that in any other kind of work."

As in Mexico, the cultivation of the sugarcane began in Brazil shortly after the Europeans settled there. The exact date is uncertain, but it may have started as early as 1516. There is some evidence that Brazilian sugar was being exported to Europe in 1519. By the 1540s sugar plantations existed all along the coastal area extending from Pernambuco in the north to São Vicente in the south. Pernambuco would

This 17th-century French engraving shows slaves laboring at an outdoor sugar mill in the Caribbean. Most sugar mills were actually inside buildings.

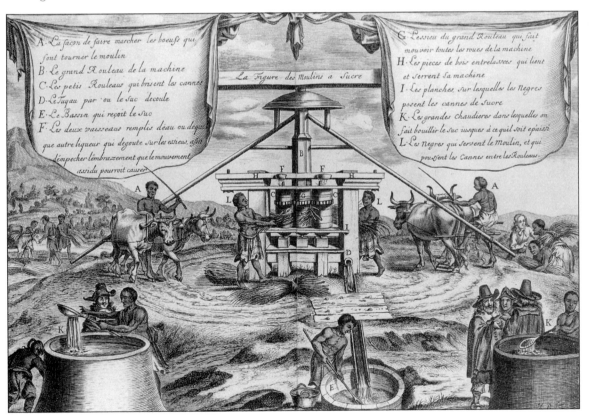

become the most important sugar-producing area in the colony by the 1580s, and by 1600 it had 200 sugar mills. In fact, by the beginning of the 17th century, Pernambuco produced more sugar than any other place in the world.

A sugar plantation in Pernambuco, Brazil, in 1640. By the 17th century, Pernambuco became the world's leading sugar-producing region.

    African slaves played an important role in the latter part of the 16th century in Pernambuco's (and Brazil's) rise to prominence in the sugar industry. It is believed that Africans first came to Brazil with the Portuguese explorer Pedro Álvares Cabral in 1500. Brazil was sparsely populated by the native peoples, and it did not, at first, appear very attractive to the Portuguese as a place to settle and accumulate wealth. A few colonists trickled in after 1500, some bringing one or two African slaves, mostly domestic servants and artisans. Not until 1539 did the

Crown receive a request from a colonist for permission to import Africans to work on his sugar plantation.

The Crown did not approve Duarte Coelhós's request, and he repeated it in 1542. This time, the colonist emphasized that the success of the sugar industry depended upon black labor. Up until that point, and for the next four or five decades, Indians provided most of the labor services on the sugar plantations. But the colonists would, at various times, press their argument that Africans were superior and hardier workers.

The first groups of slaves to arrive in Brazil directly from Africa, as opposed to being sent from Portugal, arrived at the city of Salvador in 1550. This was a momentous development, because it was the start of a formal slave trade between Brazil and Africa that would last for the next 300 years. In response to the increasing demand for African workers as a result of the expansion of the sugar industry, the Crown issued a decree in 1559 allowing the owners of sugar plantations to import a maximum of 120 slaves for each sugar mill that they owned.

This *Alvará,* or decree, gave a tremendous boost to the slave trade. Accurate records are lacking, but it is clear that Portuguese traders responded to this demand for Africans with considerable vigor. In time, African workers would replace the Indians on the plantations, and Brazil's human and cultural landscape would be irreversibly transformed. It has been estimated that after about 1580 between 10,000 and 15,000 slaves landed in Brazil annually. Most were destined to serve on the sugar plantations, and most would come from Angola.

The lot of the African on a Brazilian sugar plantation in the 16th century and later was a difficult one. With extremely hard work, long working hours, inadequate diet, and exposure to debilitating diseases, slaves faced an early death. In 1601, one commentator noted that for the slaves on the sugar plantations in Bahía, "The work is great and many die." A few years later, another observer, André João, described Brazil as "a hell for Negroes." Padre Antonio Vieira, who served in Brazil in the 17th century, left a vivid description of the conditions in a Brazilian *engenho* (sugar mill) and the experiences of the Africans who worked there:

> And truly who sees in the blackness of night those tremendous furnaces
> perpetually burning; the flames leaping from the *borbotões* [openings] of
> each through the two mouths or nostrils by which the fire breathes; the

Ethiopians or cyclopses, bathed in sweat, as black as they are strong, feeding the hard and heavy fuel to the fire, and the tools they use to mix and stir them; the cauldrons, or boiling lakes, continually stirred and restirred, now vomiting froth, exhaling clouds of steam, more of heat than of smoke. . . . the noise of the wheels and chains, the peoples of color of the very night working intensely and moaning together without a moment of peace or rest; who sees all the confused and tumultuous machinery and apparatus of that Babylon cannot doubt though they may have seen Vesuvius or Mount Etna that this is the same as Hell.

The work in the mines, *obrajes,* and sugar plantations must rank as the most demanding of the tasks that slaves had to perform in the 16th century and later. Their death rates were higher than those of slaves engaged in other tasks. This was a consequence of the terrible working conditions that prevailed in them. The sugar, mining, and textile industries were capitalist enterprises that were driven by the profit motive. Each used a combination of free and slave labor, and each depended on a great deal of labor and capital for its survival. Each was a form of industrial slavery. These enterprises, because of the need for profits, drove the slaves to their maximum, extracting as much labor from them as possible. Poorly fed and overworked, these human machines were wracked by ill health and suffered an early death.

Slaves who were used in the pearl-fishing business also faced an early death as a result of the hazardous nature of their work. They seemed to have been assigned this task in all of the coastal areas where the waters were considered particularly rich in pearls. But the divers frequently ran the risk of drowning or colliding with underwater objects. An order issued by the authorities in Vera Cruz, Mexico, in the 1550s unwittingly shows the relationship between pearl fishing and the incidence of death by drowning. The order was designed to clear the waters of sharks, not to protect the slaves. It noted that "because the bodies of drowned Negroes have not been removed from [the waters of] oyster fisheries, many sharks are present and haunt the places with grave danger to life." Given the risks involved, the colonial authorities sought to prevent Indians from pearl fishing for the colonists. In 1572, for example, Indians were forbidden to dive for pearls off the Venezuelan coast. Statistics are not available for the 16th century on the number of Africans who died while engaged in pearl fishing, but its dangerous nature was widely recognized.

African slaves were also used extensively as artisans. Many were already skilled in metalworking, cloth making, leatherwork, arts and crafts, and carpentry, to name a few skills, before they were brought to the Americas. Some acquired specialized skills in the Americas by virtue of the tasks that they were assigned. The *maestro de azúcar* (sugar master) was one of the most highly respected slaves because he was in charge of processing the cane in the *ingenios*. Such skilled workers determined the success or failure of the sugarmaking industry.

Not all colonists, whether in Brazil or Spanish America, welcomed the participation of African slaves—or even free persons—in the skilled trades. They feared that the competition from slave labor would lower the wages that they received. In addition, skilled whites wanted to confine blacks to manual labor, believing that the prestige of their trades would be lessened if they were open to slaves. As a result, several guilds that licensed tradesmen or provided specialized training excluded blacks from membership. Those that admitted blacks frequently confined them to the rank of journeyman, denying them the privilege of becoming masters.

Still, colonists who were hard-pressed for skilled labor used their slaves in a variety of capacities. Black carpenters, for example, were used extensively in the construction industry. They helped build houses, churches, monasteries, hospitals, bridges, shops, and public buildings. Others served as bricklayers, plasterers, and blacksmiths. African slaves engaged in iron working, made hats, baked bread, and sewed clothes, in addition to other skilled tasks. The image of Africans confined exclusively to field work, mining, or household chores is not accurate for the 16th or for any other century. During the 16th century most skilled slaves appear to have been located primarily in urban areas, such as Santo Domingo, Mexico City, Lima, and Salvador. Most of the European colonists were also urban residents, and they were the ones who depended on the specialized skills of the free and unfree African labor force. Black slaves and free persons were also used significantly in their households. Domestic workers, who were chiefly women, cooked, washed, cleaned, and cared for the children. Some scholars maintain that slaves in the urban areas had an easier life than those in the rural areas, particularly in the case of those who were engaged in sugar cultivation or mining. Unfortunately, we do not yet have the evidence to make any firm statements on this issue.

Not all slaves in the rural areas were agricultural workers, although most of them were during the 16th century and later. In Hispaniola,

Cuba, and Jamaica, blacks helped to grow the foods, such as maize and plantains, that sustained the islands' populations. They were also engaged in cultivating ginger on the three islands, but chiefly in Hispaniola.

There was also much diversity in the agricultural activities of the slaves on the mainland. In Mexico, for example, slaves were engaged in the cultivation of the cocoa bean in Colima, Oaxaca, and Huatulco. Others grew crops on haciendas everywhere. In Peru, slaves worked in the vineyards in the south; others grew wheat, olives, and other foodstuffs. The colonists in Venezuela used their African labor to produce cacao, cotton, vegetables, and other provisions. Most Brazilian slaves were involved in the sugar industry during the period, but some must have cultivated the crops that would feed them.

Rural slaves everywhere had to engage in pastoral activities, usually tending sheep and cattle. By 1550, the colonists in the Caribbean islands had developed a vibrant grazing economy. In Hispaniola, some families owned as many as 30,000 head of cattle by the 1540s. Slaves also worked on Mexican ranches during the 16th century, although they were not as numerous as the free workers. Slaves seem to have been more important in Peru and may even have constituted the majority of the herdsmen on some of the larger ranches. Ranching may have afforded the slaves a greater degree of control over their lives than some of the other occupations. Charged with tending livestock over huge areas of land, the slaves were quite likely free from the constant supervision of their owners.

Because slaves were expensive property, most colonists lacked the resources to purchase them. But they still needed the services of additional hands from time to time. In order to supply such colonists with the labor that they wanted, the practice of hiring out slaves developed in the 16th century. Those who needed slave labor contracted with the owners to use their human property for a fixed period of time and for a determined rental fee. As property, slaves probably had no choice in the matter; they had to go where they were sent and to work for whoever hired them.

Some people bought Africans for the sole purpose of renting them to others. The earnings from such arrangements provided them with their means of livelihood. One woman who lived in Mexico City in 1615 defended her hiring out of a slave on the grounds that "I am very poor and I have no other means of sustenance except that which the Negro

African slaves carry their master. Most slaves in the Americas performed menial tasks in households or hard labor on plantations and in mines.

earns." The economic dependence on these slaves often led to abuse. These Africans bore the burden of supporting their owners and may have had to work extremely hard to earn the money that was necessary. Felipe Guamán Poma de Ayala, who lived in Peru in the early 17th century, denounced the hiring out of slaves, claiming that they were being exploited by their owners, who were invariably women (most probably were widows). "There is no justice for the poor creatures," he wrote, "and many flee as a result." But not all owners mistreated their wage-earning slaves. Some allowed them to keep a portion of the funds that they earned, a practice that gave them a measure of economic independence. These slaves probably used the money to buy the things that they needed, and a few may even have been able to purchase their freedom, if good fortune smiled.

It appears that the slave owners in Spanish and Portuguese America assigned tasks in accordance with the gender of the workers. Males were more likely to be employed in the mining industry, in the *ingenios,* and as artisans and pearl fishers. Women were used primarily as domestics and performed the same duties as the men on the plantations. There is also some suspicion that women formed the majority of the labor force in

Two African slaves in Brazil. Carrying a basket on the head was an African tradition.

the textile factories. Because the majority of the slaves in the early period were males, women appear less frequently in the records. Historians do not yet have a clear understanding of their roles, but it is certain that the women's energies, too, went into the creation of the colonial societies in a variety of important and enduring ways.

Africans played a crucial role in building the economies of the

Americas in the 16th century. They endured the terrible conditions of the *obrajes,* the heat of the *ingenios,* and the physical hazards of the mines. Many engaged in the skilled trades and planted the food that would help feed the society as a whole. The sugar that they manufactured and the silver and other precious metals that they mined would cross the ocean to Europe with profound consequences for the diets and economies of the importing countries. The African presence would continue to grow in these societies in succeeding centuries. But the 16th-century pioneers laid the foundations of the new societies then in formation. Africans were present at the birth of the Americas as we know them today, not as colonizers but as the coerced hewers of wood and drawers of water.

CHAPTER 3
SLAVE SOCIETY AND CULTURE

E uropean colonists in every part of the Americas came to depend on the labor of Indians and Africans in the 16th century. The Indians were enslaved as soon as the Spaniards established effective control of the Caribbean islands. When Mexico, Peru, and other areas fell under Spanish control, the colonists converted the Indians on the mainland into a servile labor force. The Portuguese would do the same once they settled Brazil. In effect, the European outsiders became the ruling elite in these societies, imposing their will on the original residents and taking their land in the process. Not all of the Indians were enslaved, however. Some simply lived beyond the reach of the colonists and refused to submit to them, and in Mexico and Peru, at least in the immediate aftermath of the colonial occupation, the sheer size of the Indian population made complete control by the European conquerors impossible.

Slavery was only one of the labor systems that the Europeans employed. The Spaniards also introduced the *encomienda*. Under this system, a number of Indians were assigned by colonial authorities to work for the Spaniards without receiving wages. In return, the colonists were expected to teach the workers Spanish customs, language, and religion. These Indians were not slaves because they were not owned; the Spaniards had access only to their labor, and the condition was not

This drawing shows Indian workers in Mexico transporting weapons. Throughout Latin America, the colonists exploited native labor through slavery and the encomienda *and* repartimiento *systems. Beatings, as in the lower right, were a common form of punishment.*

hereditary. But in time, the colonists began to treat these Indians as if they were slaves, abusing them and denying them basic rights.

Faced with mounting criticism of Indian slavery and the *encomienda* system from humanitarians, the Spanish Crown abolished both in 1542. They were replaced with a system that rotated Indian workers among the Spanish colonists who needed their labor. Workers would be assigned to employers for a specified period of time, for designated tasks, and for a wage. Once the time had expired and the duties had been completed, the Indians could be allocated to other colonists. This system was called the *repartimiento* (or *mita* in Peru). It, too, proved to be an unsatisfactory response to the labor problem. Workers were often not paid, and some were held by the colonists longer than they were supposed to work.

The *repartimiento* system all but disappeared by the 17th century. In some societies, a system of debt passage emerged. Under this system, Indian workers borrowed money from their employers to purchase necessities but could not leave their job until the debt was repaid. Many people fell further and further behind because their wages were so low. Because these debts were considered hereditary, generations of Indian workers were tied to the colonists and had no option but to work for them. Not all labor services in the Spanish empire were coerced, however. Wage labor existed alongside the various unfree systems.

Like the Spanish, the Portuguese in Brazil also enslaved the Indian peoples who fell under their control. Portuguese colonists received grants of land from the Crown, under which they could enslave the Indians who resided on them. Other Indians were simply pursued, captured, and enslaved. Before 1600 almost no one doubted the right of the Portuguese colonists to treat the native peoples in this fashion. With the Indian population diminishing and the sugar industry expanding in the second half of the 16th century, Africans would come to form the dominant group of exploited workers by 1600.

Thus, Africans were not the only peoples whom the Europeans would enslave or exploit in one fashion or another. But they were the only peoples imported as permanent, unfree laborers. The 16th century was a particularly ugly one in the Americas. It saw the military defeat of the Indian peoples, their colonization, the astounding decline in their number, the introduction of oppressive labor systems, and the start of African slavery. It was a century of chaos, disaster, and crises for the native peoples. For the Africans, it was the beginning of an awful odyssey

Spanish conquistadors overwhelm a native village in the Caribbean. With the arrival of Europeans in the Americas, the native peoples suffered military defeats and a devastating loss of population and territory.

Slaves clear land on a plantation in Brazil. Brought across the Atlantic as permanent, unfree workers, African slaves helped to build the new societies of the Americas.

in these societies. Arriving as involuntary workers, African slaves confronted the challenge of helping to build societies in which they were, and would continue to be, persons with few if any rights. They also had to struggle to maintain, as best they could, a measure of human dignity, and to develop the social institutions that would sustain them.

African slaves occupied the lowest rank in the social order of the colonial societies. Imported as human property, their sole function was to work for those who had purchased them. Though the colonists valued Africans for the agricultural and craft skills that they possessed, they were nevertheless considered of "bad race" and "bad caste" by those who had come to depend on their labor. Such unflattering descriptions originated in Europe, but they assumed an added intensity and strength in the Americas as slavery expanded.

The European colonists also embraced negative images of the Indians whom they encountered. There was no inclination to see them as equals and to treat them accordingly. In fact, there was some doubt among the Spanish colonists whether the Indians were rational beings. But the pope resolved these doubts in 1537 by declaring that "the Indians are truly men."

The papal pronouncement did not lead to an end to the mistreatment of the Indians, nor did it mean that the colonists embraced them as equals. Driven by the desire to acquire wealth, the colonists wanted only

Bartolomé de las Casas, who appears as the savior of the Indians in this heroic depiction, argued that Indians were not inferior to Spaniards.

to be left alone to exploit the native peoples. Still, there were some voices raised to denounce the colonists for their behavior. Chief among them was Bishop Bartolomé de las Casas, a member of the Dominican religious order who became enraged at Spanish cruelty toward the Indians. He was not the first, however, to publicly chastise his fellow Spaniards. That honor fell to Friar Antonio de Montesinos. In 1511, he denounced the mistreatment of the Indians in Hispaniola and questioned the moral basis for their inhumane treatment.

Although the Crown introduced measures to protect the Indians, or at least reduce the level of their mistreatment, these laws were never adequately enforced. Las Casas never lost his concern for the plight of the Indian peoples and kept up an active campaign to promote their rights and reduce the degree of their exploitation. He debated one of the foremost proponents of the view that the Spaniards were superior to the Indians and were entitled to exercise control over them. This important debate was held in Valladolid, Spain, beginning in late 1550. Juan Ginés de Sepúlveda, a noted scholar, was Las Casas's opponent. The two men debated before a panel of judges and addressed the question, "What rights do the Indians have and what are the obligations of the Spaniards to them?"

A fervent admirer of the Indians, Las Casas argued that the Indians were not inferior to the Spaniards in any way. He maintained that they were "prudent and rational beings, of as good ability and judgment as other men and more able, discreet, and of better understanding than the peoples of many other nations." He believed that the Spaniards should do their own work and cease their exploitation of the Indians. Sepúlveda, on the other hand, was certain that the Spaniards were superior to the Indian peoples. The Indians lacked the capacity, he argued, to attain the level of development that the Spaniards had reached. They should be forced to work for the Spaniards and, in time, they would acquire some of the customs and habits of their superiors.

We do not know who won the debate, but the Spanish Crown seemed to have been more influenced by Las Casas's arguments. Subsequent laws were more respectful of the rights of the Indians and often limited the power of the colonists over them. Yet such laws were often not enforced, and the colonists still abused the Indians. There was a considerable difference between what the law said and how it was applied.

The debate at Valladolid and the spirit of the Spanish legislation concerning Indians underscores the fact that there was no similar concern shown by Spanish officials toward the fate of the Africans. The Indians were new peoples to the Spaniards. Africans, by contrast, had long been familiar to the Spaniards, and their image of Africans had already been framed. Even Las Casas recommended in 1517 that black slaves should be imported to replace Indian workers. He would later renounce this position.

The society that the Spaniards and the Portuguese created in the 16th century recognized racial and class distinctions. Everyone knew his

This is the title page of an English translation of a book written by Bartolomé de las Casas. In his writings and sermons, the Dominican friar (and later bishop) urged the passage of laws to protect Indians from mistreatment by Spanish colonists.

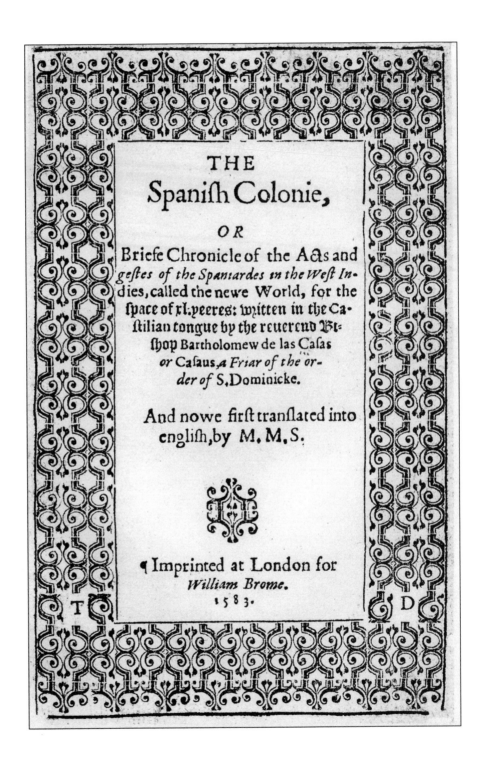

THE
Spanish Colonie,

OR

Briefe Chronicle of the Acts and *geſtes of the Spaniardes in the Weſt In-*dies, called the newe World, for the ſpace of xl.yeeres: written in the Caſtilian tongue by the reuerend Biſhop Bartholomew de las Caſas or Caſaus, *a Friar of the order of* S.Dominicke.

And nowe firſt tranſlated into engliſh, by M. M. S.

¶ Imprinted at London for
William Brome.
1583.

or her place in the social order. Whites as a group formed the elite, followed by the mixed peoples—mestizos and mulattoes. Then came the Indians and the Africans. Africans may have been set apart from the other groups because of their status as property and their racial heritage. Colonial society reserved the most difficult and hazardous jobs for Africans, sanctioned the most horrendous forms of punishment for them, and for 300 years held generations of them as property.

Black slaves consisted of three principal groups, the distinctions based primarily on the place of their birth. First, there were people who were born in Africa but spent time in Europe before they were transported to the Americas. The Spaniards called them *ladinos.* They knew some Spanish and, in varying degrees, were familiar with Spanish culture. The second category consisted of people who were born in Africa and came directly to the Americas. Known as *bozales,* these individuals

Spanish soldiers set their dogs upon a group of natives. Despite laws imposed by the Spanish Crown, cruelty against the native peoples continued in the Spanish colonies.

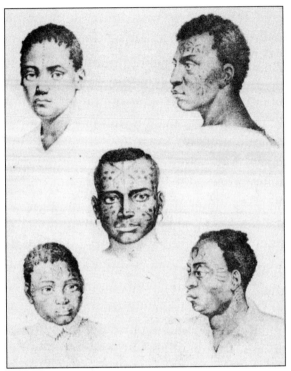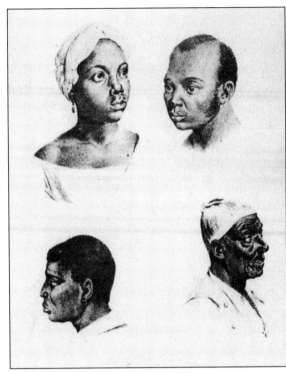

These illustrations provide portraits of slaves from Mozambique (left) and criollos, *slaves born in the Americas (right). Spanish and Portuguese colonists distinguished slaves according to where they were born.*

had little or no familiarity with the ways of the Europeans. As soon as they began to speak the languages of the Europeans and accepted Christianity, they could be called *ladinos*. The third major group of slaves comprised those who were born in the Americas. They were called *criollos* (creoles). Unlike the *bozales*, they were exposed to the cultural influences of the Europeans and other groups, such as Indians and mestizos, from birth. The *bozales* formed the majority of the slave populations once a direct slave trade with Africa was instituted in 1518. Although the *bozales* were called *ladinos* once they became accustomed to the ways of their owners, no one can say how long this process lasted. Some *bozales* probably never became *ladinos*. In any event, *ladinos* probably never lost all of their African heritage, even though they embraced aspects of the way of life in the Americas.

Early records show that the African-born slaves were renamed in the Spanish colonies and elsewhere in the Americas. These persons had no say in the selection of a new name because it was forced upon on them by the person who purchased them. In some cases, they may have been renamed by the priest who baptized them. The Africans who were renamed had to begin the difficult process of adjusting to a new identity. Their previous names had deep emotional, cultural, and ceremonial meanings, so the loss of their names must have resulted in much anguish. These Africans probably never abandoned their former names and used them among their friends and peers.

In renaming the Africans, the colonists seemed to have confined their choices to the most popular first names in usage. Thus, males were named Fernando, Juan, Jaime, Ricardo, José, Cristobal, and so on. Women were frequently called Mariá, Catarina, Luisa, Margarita, and Ana, to name just a few. Most slaves were given only one name; only a small minority had a last name, usually that of the person who owned them. In order to make their identification easier, the designation *"criollo," "ladino,"* or *"bozal"* would be listed after the slaves' names on official documents. In other cases, their ethnic or national origin would be added. Thus, official documents would list a slave as María Biafada, Ricardo Congo, or Juan Angola.

The imposition of a new name was just one of the many changes that the Africans had to endure. In order to communicate with their owners, they had to learn Spanish or Portuguese, depending on the colony. Africans spoke many different languages, but some of these languages were similar enough that the speakers could usually understand one another. In the Americas, however, the Africans had to learn the languages of the Europeans, which was the primary means of communication. Some slaves became reasonably fluent in these languages, although they probably spoke their own languages whenever possible. The African languages spoken by the slaves must also have had an impact on Spanish and Portuguese—on the vocabulary, the meanings of words, and the intonation. The slaves must have Africanized these languages, particularly in those colonies, such as Brazil, where they formed a large share of the population.

Torn from their homeland, ethnic group, family, and kin, the Africans experienced a sense of profound shock, loss, and alienation in the Americas. Kinship ties were the core of the societies from which the slaves came. Marriages united not only the husband and the wife but also the lineages to which they belonged. In most instances, the bond between the two lineages was more important than that which existed

A slave couple in Brazil converse. The Catholic church and the colonial authorities encouraged Christian marriages among African slaves.

between the couple. To be without ties of kinship was to be socially dead; an individual could exist meaningfully only as part of a network of blood relationships. The slave trade and slavery destroyed these bonds, and the individual faced the enormous challenge of re-creating them in the Americas.

The task of developing new relationships in the Americas was made more difficult by the very wide geographic distribution of the slaves in the 16th century. Few slave owners owned more than two or three Africans, although there would be very large concentrations of them in the

73

mines, *obrajes,* and on the sugar plantations as the century wore on. There were, however, enough Africans living in easy reach of one another in some places so that extensive family relationships were reconstructed by 1580. In addition, strong emotional bonds united the Africans who crossed the Atlantic in the same ship. They had endured terrible times together, and those experiences fostered strong ties among the survivors. These shipboard bonds formed the beginnings of the struggle by the Africans to create relationships among themselves and to replace those that had been severed.

As a rule, the colonial authorities did not oppose formal marriages of their slaves. In fact, the church and the state in Spain's colonies encouraged unions among the population at large, including slaves. The family was seen as the foundation stone of society. In theory, at least, once slaves were married they could not be separated through sale. Slaves whose marriages were broken up by their masters could appeal to the civil or religious authorities for redress.

This did not mean that African slaves waited for the state or the Catholic church to sanction their intimate relationships. Most slaves probably chose their partners whenever and wherever they could and had their own marriage ceremonies in accordance with their own customs and practices. Africans came from societies with complex traditions and rules that governed all aspects of human relationships, including family life, and there is no reason to believe that these were abandoned quickly, if at all, in the Americas. In their choices of marriage partners and in other ways, they responded to universal human tugs and emotions.

Beginning in the 16th century there are numerous examples of Africans getting married in Catholic ceremonies. But such marriages probably represented a minority of the unions that the slaves made. Most of them, it can be guessed, did not accept the authority of the church in this matter, because they still maintained their own traditions. Marriages that did not receive the approval of the church were, of course, considered illegal—and therefore nonexistent—by the colonial authorities.

In order to have a marriage sanctioned according to colonial rules, the Africans had to apply for a license. The prospective bride and groom had to appear with two witnesses before an official to make the request. They had to declare their ethnic backgrounds, stating whether they were Mandinka, Bram, Biafada, and so on. Creole slaves also had to indicate

Members of a slave family in Brazil work and relax outside their cabin. Slave owners sometimes disregarded the marriages of African slaves, and families were torn apart when family members were sold to other colonists.

where they were born. The witnesses had to verify the accuracy of the statements made by the couple, and they also had to state how long and under what circumstances they had known the man and woman. The authorities were not interested in whether the bride and the groom had ever been married in Africa. Such prior unions were never recognized by the church as valid because they had not occurred under Christian authority. The bride and groom had only to establish that they had never been married in the Americas or that they had been widowed.

An analysis of the surviving marriage licenses from Mexico and Peru suggests that Africans tended to marry individuals from the same ethnic group or from the same geographic area. Such a pattern of ethnically based choices should not be particularly surprising. As foreigners in strange lands, these Africans sought to reconstruct and nurture their ethnic ties and heritage. They chose partners with whom they shared a cultural heritage and who had similar life experiences. For the same reasons, creole slaves were also more likely to marry other creoles. Ethnicity, as reflected through marriage choices, remained an important part of the lives of African slaves.

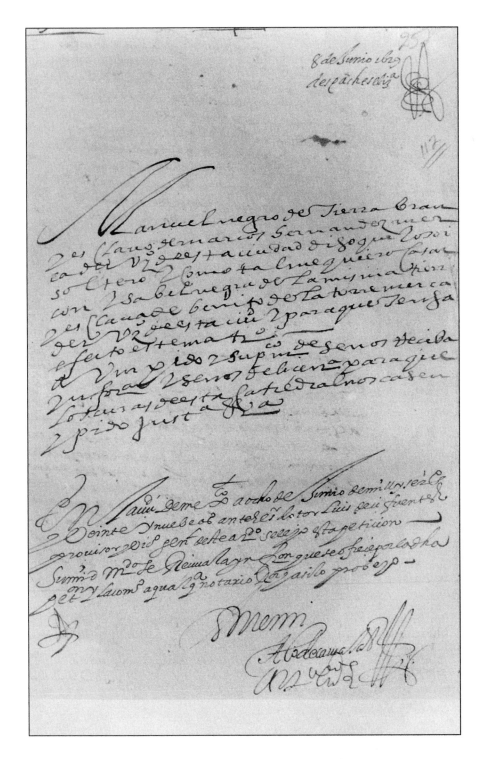

This document contains an application for marriage by two slaves whose names are at the top and a grant of permission by an official (bottom). African slaves had to make such applications to have their marriage recognized by colonial authorities.

Slave owners were not always respectful of the marriages of the Africans. The unions were sometimes broken up and families separated through sale. The church opposed such atrocities, railing against these practices from time to time but with little effect. In 1570, for example, a Mexican colonist reported to the Crown that "the *vecinos* [citizens] . . . sell some of the Negroes, which creates great inconvenience for their wives and children because they remain in this land without recourse." Some slaves, if they were aware of their rights and if they had the necessary courage, appealed to the local authorities to protect their families. But such appeals were probably not very frequent; there are only scattered references to them in the documents. In some cases, the courts ruled in favor of black litigants, but family life for Africans was never stable or free from the intrusions of outsiders.

Africans who avoided the Catholic marriage ceremonies simply lived together as man and wife, if the circumstances allowed. The Spanish colonial and religious authorities frowned on this practice, declaring it worthy of punishment. The Holy Office of the Inquisition, an institution created to pursue religious offenders of all sorts, was established in Mexico in 1570. It had been in existence in Spain for a century, and its principal targets included Jews, Muslims, and others accused of a variety of religious crimes. In Mexico, in addition to its customary victims, the Holy Office pursued blacks accused of concubinage (unmarried couples living together), bigamy (having more than one spouse), witchcraft, sorcery, and other offenses. Individuals convicted of *amancebado* (concubinage) relationships could be flogged, imprisoned, or humiliated in various ways. Bigamists received similar punishments.

By punishing those accused of bigamy and *amancebado* relationships, the Holy Office and other colonial authorities failed to understand the meanings of such behavior for the Africans. The Catholic authorities viewed church-approved marriages as the norm and refused to recognize any other form of marital arrangement as legitimate. Thus Africans who may have had their private marriage ceremonies according to their own rules ran the risk of being accused of *amancebado* and punished.

Similarly, the frequency of what the Spaniards called bigamy shows how African cultural traditions endured in the New World. It was the norm in many African societies for one man to have several wives. In others, it was acceptable if the number of women of marriageable age exceeded the number of men. Because having children was the highest service one could render in many African societies, men and women faced enormous pressure to marry and start families. If there were not enough men to go around, polygyny (having more than one wife) was a culturally proper way of solving the problem. These cultural obligations did not die in the Americas of the 16th century. African men continued to take several wives whenever that was possible. Failing to understand the larger meaning of such a practice, the colonial authorities responded in horror, broke up the unions, and punished the individuals involved. In this way they applied Western and Catholic norms to a people whose traditions and values were fundamentally different. Creoles who were accused of bigamy, particularly in the 17th century, may not have been immune to the continuing influences of their African ancestry. Judging from the testimony offered at their trials, however, some of them understood the Christian precepts against two spouses but chose to engage in that practice anyway.

Like their family arrangements, the traditional religious ideas and beliefs of the Africans were very much alive in 16th-century America. Regardless of their ethnic origins, African peoples came from societies where religious beliefs influenced all aspects of the life of individuals and the community. Unlike Western societies, there was no distinction between secular (civil) and religious spheres. Religious ideas determined the timing of important occasions, naming ceremonies, planting seasons, harvesting practices, the nature of art and dance, and a thousand other aspects of life. The African who converted to Christianity would have to undergo a profound internal rebirth as well as changes in his everyday life. In other words, the religious ideas of Africans were deeply imbedded in their human fabric, forming an central part of their being and profoundly influencing and shaping their behavior. To embrace Christianity meant, in effect, the acceptance of a new identity.

The Catholic church, with the support of the Crown and other state officials, believed that its duty was to Christianize the Africans. They had no respect for the Africans' religious ideas and practices. Muslim slaves were particularly feared, and their importation into the Americas was discouraged. The Spaniards and other Catholics had been the foes of the Muslims for centuries, and they did not want religious competition and conflicts to arise in the Americas. In addition, the Spaniards believed

Priests baptize an African man in Spain. The Spanish Crown and the Catholic church required that Africans be baptized before they were shipped to the Americas. But this rule was not always enforced.

that Muslim slaves would indoctrinate the Indians with their religious ideas.

Both the Spanish Crown and the religious authorities required that Africans be baptized prior to their departure for the Americas. It is doubtful whether this had anything more than a symbolic value because the Africans would not have received much, if any, instruction in the Catholic faith. A few slaves who came from the Congo-Angola region may have already been exposed to Christianity, because Portuguese missionaries and citizens had arrived there in the 15th century. From the complaints that the priests in the Americas made throughout the 16th century, it is clear that many slaves, contrary to what the Crown wanted, left the African coast without being baptized. The situation was not much better in the Americas. There were frequent reports that some Africans had not been baptized even after they had been in residence for several years.

This was probably a welcome development for the Africans. Undoubtedly, most of them would have preferred to continue to practice their religious beliefs without the interference of the Christians. Conscientious priests and friars, however, wanted to do their duty as Christians to instruct the Africans about their faith and to baptize them. With the permission of the owners, they conducted classes for the slaves on Sundays or at other mutually convenient times. Not all slaveholders cooperated, some believing that the time that their human property spent receiving religious instructions should be devoted to working at their various tasks.

Still, many Africans were baptized and became formal members of the church. They participated in the various festivals and had marriages and funerals performed by a priest. Some Africans became active members of the religious brotherhoods known as the *cofradía*. In essence, these were mutual aid organizations that were devoted to the memory of a particular saint. The members paid dues and received financial help in times of difficulty. *Cofradías* took part in the various religious processions that occurred from time to time.

The authorities in the colonies kept a careful watch on the activities of black *cofradías*. The spectacle of hundreds of blacks congregating to hold meetings or to participate in processions raised white fears of conspiracy and insurrection. In 1572, for example, the Mexican viceroy was concerned that "recently the negroes have had a *cofradía* and have assembled and held processions with their members as the others do, and these are always increasing...and it seems that they may create problems." On occasion, intoxicated members did create problems in Mexico and Peru and probably elsewhere. In 1612, members of a black *cofradía* in Mexico City played a leading role in a rebellion that slaves and free persons had planned. Such rebellious activity led to the temporary suspension of the organization by the authorities. The potential of the *cofradías* to lead violent assaults on slavery must have led to an increase

Two Catholics of African descent worship in Peru. Many Africans became formal members of the Catholic church in Latin America.

in their surveillance. In general, however, *cofradías* were more likely to meet the needs of the slaves for social interaction and communal activities.

The first black *cofradías* may have been established as soon as enough Africans were baptized in a particular colony and lived close to one another. The church encouraged the formation of separate *cofradías* for Africans, probably for racial reasons. The Africans may also have wanted their own organizations, free from the direct control of whites and reflecting their own needs and bearing their cultural stamp. In fact, the *cofradías* in Peru, and perhaps in other colonies as well, were organized along African ethnic lines in the 16th century. This could only have occurred in those places where individuals from particular ethnic groups existed in significant numbers. The existence of ethnic-based *cofradías* clearly suggests the continuing strength of an African heritage in the Americas.

Although the Catholic church succeeded in making converts among the slaves, Christianity did not replace African religious beliefs in the 16th century or at later times. Christianized Africans did not abandon their core religious beliefs. In other words, their African religious ideas existed alongside the dogma of the Christianity that they embraced. African slaves could draw upon their Christian beliefs when it suited their purposes. On other occasions, they drew upon their African beliefs.

The Holy Office of the Inquisition persecuted those who practiced African religions in Mexico and Peru, and church authorities everywhere also denounced them. Modern historians have frequently dismissed African-inspired religious beliefs as "superstitions." Scholars and students, however, should not characterize or pass judgment on the ideas of the peoples whose history they study. The goal is to understand these ideas and the roles that they played in individual lives and in society. Western scholars have too frequently failed to respect the ideas of other peoples, dismissing them in negative terms. The Africans, for the most part, were not Christians. They shared other religious ideas, and their belief systems should be studied on their own terms and not through the cultural lens of Christians and Westerners.

Practitioners of African religions used a variety of charms and amulets in their rituals. These could be herbs, sticks, bags, cloth, or bones. Africans believed that these objects carried certain mystical powers or were the objects through which the supernatural operated. Dirt from cemeteries, perhaps because of its association with the ancestors, also possessed revered qualities. When used in the appropriate fashion and accompanied by the relevant ceremonies, the charms, objects, and dirt could be used to avenge a wrong, win the affections of a man or woman, solve a crime, get a slave owner to treat his slaves well, and accomplish a variety of other objectives.

The use of these objects and charms was based on the belief that certain forces or events could be manipulated and controlled by resorting

Slaves in Brazil perform a traditional dance. Africans carried many elements of their cultures to the Americas, including music, dance, art, and cooking methods.

to the appropriate ritual acts. This is similar in some respects to the Christian belief that prayer can be used effectively to achieve a desired end. What is important, however, is not any perceived similarity to Christianity, but the persistence of African beliefs and ways of influencing the supernatural in the Americas. Over time, of course, some of these ideas and practices would be modified or altered in some fashion.

In addition to their kinship systems and religious ideas, Africans brought their music, songs, dances, art forms, and cooking methods with them. The colonists viewed many of these cultural practices negatively, and tried to suppress them. Slaves danced in the streets on festive

occasions, drawing upon their African styles of movement. Others were skilled at drumbeating and played such stringed musical instruments as the banjo and marimba.

We possess little information on the diet of the slaves during their early years in the Americas. The principal ingredients appear to be corn, sweet potatoes, plantains, beef, and a variety of legumes (beans). The nutritional adequacy of the diet is also unknown because of the absence of information about the quantity of the foods provided to each slave. Similarly, we can make no definite comment on the relationship between diet, disease, and the death rates of the slaves. Slaves, like other members of society, fell victim to the frequent epidemics of measles and smallpox. Workers in the mines and the *ingenios* had a higher death rate than other blacks, a result of the physical hazards of such employment and perhaps of overwork and a poor diet. The unhealthy climate of such places as Vera Cruz may also have taken its toll on the health of the slaves.

Medical care, such as it was, was available for sick slaves, particularly those who lived in urban areas. In Lima, for example, a hospital run

Slaves brought the banjo to the Americas, where playing African music was one way of preserving their culture. This mid-19th-century banjo is from Baltimore, Maryland.

by the Jesuits welcomed slaves and gave them the same care that they provided to whites. Hospitals run by municipalities also accepted slaves in Mexico City and Lima. Some large plantations in the rural areas had infirmaries attached to them. Given the state of medical knowledge during the 16th century, it is doubtful whether these hospital stays did any good if serious illnesses were involved. African slaves had their own traditional remedies, and many of them may not have availed themselves of the services that the hospitals offered. They also seemed to have borrowed freely from the medical lore of the Indians. This is hardly surprising, given their often close interaction with one another.

Indians and Africans also fell in love with each other, got married, or lived together without the approval of the church or the state. The Spanish Crown, in particular, opposed such unions, preferring that individuals choose partners from among their own "races" or groups. But such a restriction was impossible to enforce. Male Africans greatly outnumbered the females, so Indian women often became the sexual partners of black men. Because the Indian women were likely to be free, the children of such unions, known as *zambos,* took the mother's legal status and were born free. This was probably an added incentive for male slaves to choose Indian women as partners.

The early colonial records indicate, however, that there was some tension in the relationship between the Africans and the native peoples of the Americas. It may very well be that colonial officials focused much more on the difficulties between them, ignoring the many areas and instances of cooperation. In particular, the Peruvian and Mexican authorities accused blacks of physically assaulting Indians, taking their possessions, and generally mistreating them.

In order to correct this problem, the Crown and the local authorities attempted to prevent the two peoples from living in the same communities. These restrictions were sometimes not enforced, and they were repeated with regularity throughout the 16th century. The Crown also forbade blacks from trading with Indians on the grounds that they took advantage of them. It is doubtful, however, that the commercial activity between the two groups ceased.

The apparent uneasy relationship that existed between the Indians and the Africans is difficult to understand. Some scholars have suggested that the situation was the result of a colonial policy that sought to divide

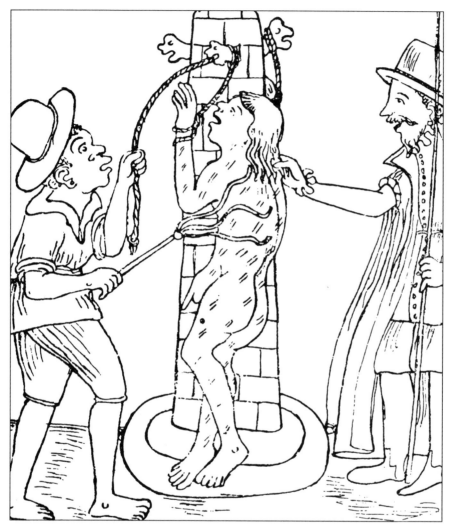

Under the direction of a Spanish colonist, a black slave flogs an Indian. The relationship between Indians and Africans was strained, perhaps because of cultural differences and the efforts of colonists to set the two groups against each other.

the two peoples and promote mutual hostility between them, thereby making it easier to govern them. There may be some validity to this conclusion. There were, however, enormous cultural differences between the different African ethnic groups, and the Indian populations were also ethnically divided. These cultural differences did not produce mutual understanding and tolerance. One result was hostility and violence. Africans may also have been upset—and understandably so—when Indians joined the colonists to suppress slave revolts or destroy communities of runaways.

Regardless of the colony in which they lived, Africans were placed at the bottom of the social order. Forced to work for others, they nevertheless tried to maintain their humanity, doing the things that gave meaning to their lives. They toiled, married, reproduced, worshiped their gods, and made the best of their situation. Their burdens were never easy, and the forced separation from their homeland created much physical suffering and emotional anguish. But those Africans who arrived in the 16th century faced, in retrospect, an additional challenge. It was they who had to lay the cultural and institutional foundations of the modern black societies of the Americas.

CHAPTER 4
THE STRUGGLE FOR FREEDOM

In this 18th-century engraving, a cimarron *warrior carries a musket as he goes into battle in Suriname. Individually and in organized groups, African slaves and their descendants resisted slavery until the institution finally came to an end throughout the Americas in the 19th century.*

The resistance to slavery in the Americas was a continuation of the struggles that many people had waged on the African coast as they awaited the departure of the slave ships. Although the evidence is scant for the early years, the captives must also have fought to free themselves during the Atlantic passage, much as other Africans would do in a later period. These people participated in rebellions, jumped overboard, engaged in hunger strikes, and challenged the authority of the ships' crews in a variety of ways. Many of the enslaved not only rejected their physical condition but also refused to allow their spirits to be crushed by their awful predicament.

The experiences and emotions of the slaves during the middle passage can never be fully recaptured. The anguish of being involuntarily separated from their kin, culture, and familiar surroundings must have been very great, regardless of their age. Not only did these persons have to adjust to the demands of their servile condition, but they also had to try to maintain their mental balance as well. These were extraordinarily difficult challenges, and it is a wonder that so many of them survived physically and were able to maintain some degree of emotional health.

Still, the individuals who made up the slave cargoes in these early years must have had a special kind of fortitude and inner strength. During the 16th and early 17th centuries, the journey from Africa to the

89

ports in the Caribbean and Latin America could last up to five months. Death and disease took their steady toll, and the physical conditions under which the human cargoes traveled tested their capacity for suffering and abuse. Many of the survivors arrived sick and terrified, their bodies and souls reeling from the ordeal that they had endured.

Perhaps the Africans could have eased their emotional pain in that terrible first century if they had been present in larger numbers in the various colonies. This would have provided them with the opportunity to associate more intimately with one another and establish meaningful support systems. But even when relatively large numbers of slaves arrived in such colonies as Mexico, Peru, and Hispaniola, they were widely scattered. Most lived in small groups of their peers. Not until the mid 17th century did the large sugar plantations, with their huge concentrations of slaves, become increasingly regular features of the Caribbean islands. The silver mines of Mexico and Peru and a few sugar plantations had employed high numbers of slaves before 1600, but most blacks still lived in smaller communities.

An African population living in larger groups would not have automatically ended the alienation that its members felt or have fostered a sense of community among them. The African-born slaves were divided along ethnic lines, which was an obstacle to cooperative relationships between them and the development of a sense of oneness. In addition, there were cultural differences between those people who had become familiar with the ways of Europeans and those who were newly arrived from Africa bearing their traditional culture.

Thus, the slave population had to overcome many obstacles before it could pose an organized challenge to the institution under whose control it lived. Such challenges took different forms, depending on the local circumstances, the size of the slave population, the degree of interaction among its members, and their level of political consciousness. Slaves who lived within easy reach of wooded, mountainous, or other inaccessible areas often chose flight as their principal means of resistance. Where their numbers permitted, others conspired and participated in revolts. Still others engaged in day-to-day acts of sabotage, such as working slowly, that punctured the efficiency of the institution of slavery.

Slaves were inclined to resist their condition when they came to the recognition that a profound wrong had been committed against them. Resistance occurred when the individual had decided to reclaim control

A slave owner disciplines a slave by hitting her palms with a stick. Such incidents of punishment sometimes provoked slaves to make risky attempts to gain their freedom.

over his or her life. Such a decision could come after much careful thought, or it could occur in a moment of passion, such as when the person was being mistreated. Once a decision to resist had been made, whether individually or collectively, the slave had reached an important turning point, and his or her life would not be the same again.

During the 17th century, when black cultures in the Americas were taking firm shape, slaves engaged in flight more frequently than any other form of physical resistance. This was the case in all of the colonies, and there were several reasons for its appeal. Regardless of whether the slaves were shipped from Spain or came directly from Africa, the overwhelming majority were African-born. They were, therefore, unaccustomed to the demands and rigors of plantation, mining, and other forms of labor that they were required to perform. Not surprisingly, they sought to escape from the sources of their oppression as soon as the opportunity presented itself. Often few in numbers and separated from their peers by long distances, flight also had a certain practicality. It did not depend significantly on the cooperation of others for its success. Slaves could escape alone or in a group. Small groups were best because slaves ran the risk of detection and capture if the number in the escape party was too large.

The physical environment of the colonies also aided escape. Hispaniola, Jamaica, Cuba, Mexico, and Brazil, to name just a few places, all had mountainous, inaccessible, and wooded areas—the ideal terrain for those who wanted to create sanctuaries away from their pursuers. The Sierra Maestra mountain range in eastern Cuba, the densely wooded Cockpit Country in central Jamaica, the hilly Orizaba zone adjacent to Vera Cruz in Mexico, and the densely forested regions of northeastern Brazil beckoned and protected the escapees.

Adult males were the most likely to escape. Women constituted a minority of the slave population, so it is not surprising that they remained a small proportion of those who fled. Perhaps women were less inclined to risk the hazards of the escape than the men. They may also have chosen to remain behind with their children. Because infants and older children slowed the pace of escape and increased the risk of capture, parents had to face difficult choices in this regard.

The incidence of escape began as soon as the first slaves arrived in Hispaniola in 1502. In 1503, the governor of the colony, Nicolás de Ovando, reported to the Crown that a number of slaves had fled. There is no additional information on this first group of runaways, but they probably fled to a remote area of the colony. Whatever their fate, these people established a pattern that would be followed by other slaves everywhere in the Americas.

These escaped slaves were called *cimarrones* by the Spaniards. The origin of this term is not entirely clear, but some scholars believe that the word *cimarrón* originally referred to cattle that roamed in the hills of Hispaniola. Eventually, it was applied to Indians who had fled from slavery. As Indian slavery declined and blacks arrived in increasing numbers, the word came to be associated with those who escaped. It is not certain, however, when *cimarrón* began to be applied exclusively to black runaways, but it appears that was the case by the 1530s. In time, the English equivalent became *maroon,* and the French used the word *marron.* The word *cimarrón,* at least in the eyes of the Spaniards, had negative connotations. It was generally a synonym for "wild," "fierce," or "untamed." On the other hand, the escapees may have worn it as a badge of honor, in the same way that the descendants of the maroons in the English-speaking Caribbean do today.

There was a close relationship between the number of escapes and the size of the black population. As more and more Africans arrived, the

Attended by a slave, this flamboyantly dressed hidalgo, or nobleman, was typical of the Spanish adventurers who flocked to the Americas in search of wealth. The Spaniards later became the targets of attacks by escaped slaves, known as cimarrones.

flight to an uncertain freedom in the mountains and other remote areas accelerated. Slaves who were inclined to escape probably ran off quietly, perhaps not even telling friends of their plans for fear of betrayal. The colonists may even have come to expect that some of their slaves would flee. The surviving documents from these early years often mention *cimarrones* in an offhand manner. It is only when the escaped slaves began to attack their former masters or entice other slaves to escape that their existence became a matter of grave public concern.

It was not until the 1520s that the references to *cimarrones* in the letters of the colonists and in official reports became more frequent and urgent. There were reports of *cimarrones* not only in Hispaniola, but also in Mexico in 1523, in Puerto Rico in 1529, and in Cuba in 1534. By the 1550s, additional reports of the presence of *cimarrones* had come from Panama, Venezuela, Peru, and Honduras. In general, the *cimarrones* were accused of murdering Spaniards, participating in rebellions, and theft. In 1546, a Spanish official in Hispaniola, for example, noted that the *cimarrones* in one part of the island were so dangerous that "no one dared to venture out unless he was in a group of fifteen to twenty people." In Lima, the authorities complained that the *cimarrones* "go about robbing the travelers on the roads . . . and the natives." The same authorities claimed in 1549 that the runaways were "committing many robberies and murders."

Colonial authorities everywhere saw the *cimarrones* as a threat to public order. As a result, the descriptions of them in the records are overwhelmingly negative. Given the fact that the *cimarrones* in all of the colonies were depicted as assaulting the colonists and, in some cases, the Indians, such charges must have had some merit. Because such accusations were often followed by requests for resources to strengthen the law-enforcement agencies, it is also conceivable that the reports gave exaggerated accounts of the behavior of the escapees.

It is important to understand why the *cimarrones* escaped and sometimes attacked the colonists. These were human beings who had become slaves and who were abused and denied the right to shape their own destinies. Their escape was a rejection of their enslaved condition and a courageous attempt to claim control over their own lives. Lacking any loyalty to the society that oppressed them, they engaged in acts that outraged those who controlled and benefited from their enslavement. Thus, the white colonists were the principal targets of these assaults. The *cimarrones* and their actions represented the first sustained threats to the institution of slavery in the hemisphere. As a result, they must be given a special place in the history of the struggles of the peoples of African descent for freedom and social justice in the Americas.

Some historians have attempted to make distinctions between the motivations of the *cimarrones* and those who remained in slavery but participated in revolts. They suggest that the *cimarrones* did not pose

This 1671 engraving provides an early view of Mexico City. In such urban areas, slaves were more likely to organize rebellions because their population was denser than in rural areas.

much of a threat to slavery because they escaped from the institution and returned only now and then to carry out hit-and-run attacks on it. On the other hand, slave revolts threatened slavery from within and were designed to destroy it. This distinction does not hold for the early years, when *cimarrones* played the most significant roles in a large number of the early challenges to slavery.

With the possible exception of a few urban areas such as Mexico City and Lima, slaves were so sparsely distributed in the 16th century that they lacked the numbers necessary to organize and launch rebellions. Slaves apparently escaped individually or in small groups and eventually formed maroon communities of varying sizes. In 1542, one estimate in Hispaniola placed the number of *cimarrones* at "about 2,000 or 3,000." Several hundred were reported to be in Puerto Rico at various times in the 16th century. The same could be said of Mexico, particularly in the mountainous area between Mount Orizaba and Vera Cruz. Accounts from Peru, Cuba, and Venezuela also suggest significant runaway populations in those early years.

The existence of these communities gave the *cimarrones* the confidence to challenge the slave owners and their colonial society. The *cimarrones* were, for the most part, interested not only in preserving their own freedom, but in destroying slavery as well. The first slave rebellion in the Americas occurred in Hispaniola in 1522. Three years earlier, in 1519, Indians were reported to have been joined by escaped slaves in an attack on the Spaniards. But when the first all-black revolt occurred in 1522, it included *cimarrones* and slaves who had never fled. The 40 slaves and *cimarrones* who participated were, however, defeated by the Spaniards. Several lost their lives in the fighting, and the Spaniards hanged those who were captured.

This early assault on the Spaniards was followed by others. It is doubtful, however, that the runaways always united with the slaves. Nor is it entirely clear if all of the disturbances were designed to destroy slavery or whether they were a consequence of the *cimarrones* defending their communities from invasions by the Spanish authorities. It is certain, nonetheless, that there were serious confrontations between the Spaniards and the *cimarrones* in Puerto Rico in 1529; Cuba in 1534; Mexico, Columbia, Hispaniola in the 1540s; and Panama in the 1550s.

The Mexican *cimarrones* were probably the most active during the 16th and early 17th centuries. Mexico's slave population steadily increased after the Spanish occupation, and the native peoples declined in number. There were about 20,000 African slaves in Mexico by 1570 and perhaps as many as 50,000 by 1600. The Mexican terrain, with its numerous mountain slopes, provided ideal sanctuaries for escaped slaves. The number of escapes increased after the 1550s, and there were frequent reports from the silver mines in the north and the east that *cimarrones* were engaged in attacks on the colonists. In some cases, Indians joined the *cimarrones* in acts of arson and theft. By 1580, *cimarrones* could be found almost everywhere in rural Mexico.

Relatively speaking, a great deal is known about a community of *cimarrones* that lived in the area of Mount Orizaba adjacent to Vera Cruz during the late 16th and early 17th centuries. The community had developed a reputation for attacking the Spaniards, taking their possessions, and enticing other slaves to flee. Their leader was Yanga, an African-born man who had escaped shortly after arriving in Mexico. Evidently a skilled military tactician, he had successfully repulsed several attempts by the Spaniards to destroy his settlement and return the residents to slavery. By 1608 there were about 500 *cimarrones* in the community. They supported themselves by planting such crops as corn and potatoes and by rearing animals.

Despite their best efforts, the *cimarrones* were unable to withstand an aggressive assault on their camp in 1609. An invading army of 450 men forced Yanga and his people to accept a truce. Under the terms of the agreement, the Spanish authorities recognized the freedom of the *cimarrones* and allowed them to establish and govern their own town. Yanga would become governor of the town, and the position could only be held by those descended from him. The *cimarrones* promised to defend the colony if it were ever attacked by Spain's enemies and agreed to return all future runaways to their owners. It is not clear whether this part of the agreement was kept. In accordance with the terms of the agreement, the town of San Lorenzo de los Negros received its charter in 1617.

The treaty that these *cimarrones* signed with the Spanish set a model for other societies. In later years, maroons signed peace treaties with the authorities in Jamaica, Cuba, Suriname, Venezuela, and other places. Many of these large maroon communities came into existence after 1600. In Jamaica, for example, one group of maroons signed a peace treaty with the English in 1739 that affirmed their freedom. Similar treaties would be signed with other maroon groups in succeeding years.

The slaves in Brazil also embraced escape as an effective form of resistance. As early as 1597 a Jesuit priest complained that the "foremost enemies of the colonizers are revolted Negroes from Guiné in some mountain areas, from where they raid and give much trouble, and the time will come when they will dare to attack and destroy farms." Portuguese assaults on some of these settlements killed many of the residents but failed to destroy them. The most resilient of these early maroons were those who established a settlement known as Palmares in Pernambuco. In 1612 a Portuguese official noted that "some 30 leagues inland, there is a site between mountains called Palmares which harbors

SOULEVEMENT DES NEGRES
à la Jamaïque.

Cimarrones kill colonists in a revolt against the English in 1758. Starting in the early 17th century, large communities of escaped slaves were powerful enough to sign peace treaties with colonial authorities in Mexico, Jamaica, and other colonies.

runaway slaves . . . whose attack and raids force the whites into armed pursuits which amount to little for they return to raid again."

Palmares had between 11,000 and 20,000 residents at its peak in the 17th century. After maintaining their freedom for almost a century, however, the residents of the settlement were finally defeated by the

Portuguese in 1694. The disappearance of Palmares as an organized community of maroons did not end this form of resistance in Brazil. Known as *quilombos,* such settlements became more numerous as the slave population increased. Some of these communities still survive in contemporary Brazil.

Slave owners and the colonial authorities attempted to curb the incidence of runaways. Several colonies, such as Mexico and Peru, established civil militias primarily to catch runaways and prevent their attacks on Spanish life and property. In addition, the authorities introduced a series of measures for the punishment of those who escaped and were recaptured. Some of these laws permitted the castration of the *cimarrones* and even authorized their deaths if they had escaped for long periods of time. According to a 1535 law passed in Lima, an absence of more than six days carried the death penalty. Runaways could also be whipped, chained, imprisoned, tortured, or have a foot or hand cut off. Such horrible punishments reflected the seriousness with which the authorities viewed the slaves' efforts to claim their freedom. On the other hand, by escaping in the face of such reprisals, the slaves demonstrated the powerful nature of their desire to live as free people.

Although the *cimarrones* and the slaves who did not flee joined together sometimes to challenge slavery, there were occasions on which this was evidently not the case. In fact, several slave revolts during this early period and later do not appear to have involved the participation of *cimarrones.* There were organizational difficulties that stood in the way of such collaboration. Maroons lived in remote areas, and communication between them and the slaves was usually not easy. Nor should it be assumed that the *cimarrones* always wanted to involve themselves in such conflicts. They had fled from slavery; the struggle to destroy it remained the primary responsibility of those who were left behind.

The first major conspiracy involving slaves acting alone occurred in Mexico City in 1537. The conspirators elected a king and planned to kill the Spaniards, liberate themselves, and seize control of the colony. The plot, however, was discovered by the authorities, and those involved were arrested. A frightened government extracted confessions from the accused and hanged them. The threat of rebellion never declined in Mexico, and the Spaniards always feared that the Indians would join the black slaves in any confrontation. As one English traveler noted in 1573, "The Indians and the Negroes daily wait, hoping to put in practice their freedom from the domination and the servitude in which the Spaniards keep them. Indians and Negroes hate and abhor the Spaniards with all their hearts."

Spanish fears were fulfilled in 1608 when 31 free blacks and slaves gathered in Mexico City to elect a king and queen and to plot a revolt. One of the conspirators reported the details to the authorities. Predictably, the participants were arrested, although it is not clear what punishment they received. Four years later, in 1612, blacks in Mexico City once again planned a revolt. When the authorities heard of the plans they arrested a large number of people and tortured them to obtain more information on the conspiracy. In the end, 35 blacks were hanged and others were sent out of the colony.

Slave conspiracies and revolts were, of course, not confined to Mexico. In 1552, the black slaves and some Indians who labored in the silver mines at Buria, Venezuela, revolted. Miguel, their leader, justified their behavior on the grounds that "God had created them as free as any other people in the world." The slaves who were engaged in pearl fishing on the small island of Margarita, just off the Venezuelan coast, also rebelled in 1603. The only surviving account of the incident noted that "a great quantity of Negro slaves" rose, but the details are scanty. Led by a woman who invoked supernatural powers that she was believed to possess, the rebellion failed, and the woman was seized and beheaded.

Slaves continued to escape in all societies of the Americas, and many were successful in building their own communities and maintaining their freedom. Maroon communities united slaves from different African ethnic groups as well as the creoles. The first settlements, however, consisted almost exclusively of African-born persons. These communities probably saw the breaking down of ethnic divisions as the Ibos, the Coromantee, the Mandinka, and others had to cooperate with one another in order to survive. These communities of runaway slaves represented the first truly black societies in the Americas. Free from white control and responsible for their own decisions, these societies were the first attempts by African peoples in this hemisphere to order their lives in their own way. Their societies were always insecure, however, because they faced the constant threat of invasions from the outside. Yet many of them survived for long periods of time because the desire for freedom gave them the necessary resolve to confront, and in many cases overcome, the obstacles that stood in their path.

The communities that these maroons established appear to have been patterned along the lines of African societies. Although information on this subject is still rather sketchy, such communities could be characterized as centralized kingdoms with a ruler, such as Yanga, wielding absolute or near-absolute power. These communities, of course, were also influenced by the conditions the escapees encountered in the Americas. Consequently, they were never exact copies of the Africa that they remembered. In any event, the maroons created communities that met their needs and bore their own cultural and political stamp.

No slave revolt, however, achieved any success during this first century. The slaves could not successfully contest the armed might of the colonial states. Not until two centuries later were slaves in Haiti able to claim their freedom through their own efforts. Still, the incidence of revolts and conspiracies shows that the enslaved never resigned themselves to their condition and never saw it as just. Although relatively few in number, these individuals gave slave owners everywhere notice that they could never be taken for granted.

The enslavement of the African peoples in the Americas finally ended in 1888. In that year, Brazil became the last society to emancipate its slaves, bringing to an end a process that had begun in the first decades of the 19th century. The Haitian slaves began a successful revolution in 1791 and finally defeated the French slave-owning colonists in 1803. When they achieved their independence from Spain in the early 19th century, the former Spanish colonies began a slow process of liberating their slaves. The British passed an Emancipation Act in 1833, and the French followed suit in 1848. In North America, all of the slaves were freed in 1865 as a result of a bloody civil war. Puerto Rico ended the institution in 1873, and Cuba acted similarly in 1886.

There were, of course, a number of slaves who managed to become legally free before slavery formally ended in the various societies. This process began in the 16th century, but its extent varied, depending on the society and the forces that encouraged freedom for some slaves. In all of the slaveholding societies of the Americas, a child born to a free woman but fathered by a male slave was legally free. Some slave owners freed their own children born of slave women and sometimes those women as well. Others liberated slaves who had grown too old to work or who had served faithfully for a period of time. Some slaves purchased their freedom; others had it done on their behalf by a sympathetic citizen

DON P. Z.Z.A.S.   DON FRAN. DEA ROBE. 56. A   DÔDOMÍNGO. 18 A

or humanitarian. Children born to parents who were already free also added to the size of the free black population.

The Spanish legal code, the *Siete Partidas,* encouraged liberty for slaves. It stated that slavery was "the most evil and the most despicable thing that can be found among men." As a result, according to the *Siete Partidas,* "all of the laws of the world should lead toward freedom." Owners who freed their slaves, the document maintained, rendered a service to God. In 1540, the Crown echoed these sentiments and advised its officials in the Americas that if slaves "should publicly demand their liberty, they should be heard and justice done to them, and care be taken that they should not on that account . . . be maltreated by their Masters." There was, of course, a tremendous gulf between these ideals and actual practice both in Spain and in the colonies. The Portuguese never produced a document similar to the *Siete Partidas* and did not embrace, at least in legal theory, the notion that property in persons was not to be encouraged.

The existence of the *Siete Partidas* and its strictures against slavery, as we have seen, did not prevent the enslavement of large groups of people, either in Spain or in the American colonies. It was an ideal that Spaniards never attained. The racial origins of the slave population in the Americas made it easier for the Spaniards to enslave them without a guilty conscience.

Wearing Spanish clothes and native jewelry, zambos *from Esmeraldas (in present-day Ecuador) visit Quito in 1599. Some* zambos, *children of blacks and Indians, were among the many free Africans in the Americas.*

Seen against this background, the enslavement of the Africans in the Americas was not an issue about which 16th-century Spaniards and Portuguese worried. Only a few enlightened voices raised questions about the morality of African slavery, but their objections had no effect. One of the first people to do so was Alonso de Montufár, the archbishop of Mexico. In 1560 he wrote to the king of Spain complaining that "we do not know what reason exists that the Negroes should be enslaved more than the Indians . . . because they receive the holy faith and do not make war against the Christians." Nine years later, Friar Tomás de Mercado denounced the abuses of the slave trade and urged his fellow Spaniards not to participate in it. In 1573, Bartolomé de Albornoz, a professor who lived in Mexico, wrote a well-known treatise condemning slavery. He pointed out that the institution violated natural law, or the basic "natural" rights of all human beings. These were lonely voices; it was not until the second half of the 18th century that a movement to abolish the slave trade—and eventually slavery—gathered momentum, particularly in England and France.

The slaves who gained their freedom in the 16th century, therefore, benefited from individual arrangements and not from any formal end of slavery. While some slaves were freed by their owners, others worked hard, saved whatever money came their way and, if the master were agreeable, bought their freedom. On occasion, slaves could not readily meet the price the master asked, so they purchased their freedom over a period of years.

The purchase of one's freedom on the installment plan seemed to have begun quite early in the 16th century. One of the first examples took place in Mexico in 1544. A woman entered into a contract to buy her freedom and that of her daughter for 210 pesos. The agreement required that she pay 60 pesos at the outset and the remainder in installments. Mother and daughter would receive their freedom when the final payment was made. There are other examples of the extraordinary sacrifice that slaves would make to purchase their liberty. The irony involved in having to purchase the freedom of one's self and one's children could hardly have been lost on either the owner or the owned.

Young men between the ages of 14 and 25 were the group least likely to be freed. They were in the most productive years of their lives physically, and slave owners were not particularly eager to part with their strongest and healthiest workers. At the other extreme, the mulatto children of the slave masters and the mistresses of these men stood the best chance of acquiring their freedom. Liberty was clearly not within the reach of everyone in quite the same way. Most African-born slaves and their children, it should be said, could expect to spend their entire lives in bondage.

Individuals who received their freedom had to have it formally enshrined in a document. This gave them protection against reenslavement and indicated the terms under which they were freed. The document noted whether freedom came as a result of purchase, and if so, the amount of money that was involved. It also indicated the date when the person's freedom came into effect, as well as whether there were conditions attached to it. In some cases, slave owners required that the freed person continue to work for them or their heirs, but for a wage.

It is impossible to say how many persons received their freedom in the Spanish empire and in Portuguese Brazil in the 16th century. The proportions probably never exceeded 5 percent to 10 percent of the black population at any time. It may be guessed, however, that the number of freed persons in the Spanish colonies increased steadily after 1550 simply because of the continuing growth of the black population, the incidence of owners freeing their children and mistresses, and the fact that some slaves by that time had been in the colonies long enough and received their freedom because of advancing age.

There were no laws in the colonies that prevented slaves from being freed. This did not mean, however, that free blacks were accorded equal rights with whites. The white colonists dominated the colonies, and blacks and Indians, regardless of their legal status, occupied subordinate places. The free peoples of African descent were expected to pay taxes, serve in the armed forces, and generally assume the responsibilities of full citizenship, but they were the victims of discriminatory legislation because of their racial heritage.

As soon as the numbers of free blacks began to increase, the Spanish Crown and the colonial authorities sought to control their lives and limit their opportunities. Such actions were based on the racist notion that blacks needed white supervision. Unlike the slaves, free blacks could, at least in theory, choose their employers and move from place to place. The colonists feared the loss of control over them, as well as loss of access to their labor. Beginning in the 1570s free blacks were ordered to live with Spaniards and work for them for a wage. This was a serious

Black carpenters construct a boat. Many free blacks in the Americas were skilled artisans, such as carpenters, but they did not enjoy the same civil liberties as whites.

curtailment of their liberty and made them little better than slaves. Other measures required that all freed persons be registered with the local authorities in order to make it easier to collect taxes from them. Failure to be registered brought severe physical punishments. The order was repeated from time to time, an indication that some free persons successfully evaded it.

Most free blacks performed menial and unskilled tasks during the period, but some were artisans much in demand. The various guilds— associations of craftsmen, such as carpenters—either refused membership to free blacks or allowed them to become only apprentices. They were also excluded from high schools and universities, a fact that also limited their economic and social opportunities.

The Spanish-American societies went to extraordinary lengths throughout the period to emphasize the inferior status of the free persons of African descent. In 1614, for example, the authorities in Lima ruled that free blacks should be buried without coffins. Evidently, burial in a coffin blurred the social distinctions between whites and blacks. The authorities in Mexico and Peru also prevented free black women from adorning themselves with gold and other jewelry and wearing silk. Such finery was the preserve of white women, as a mark of their social superiority.

Freed persons appear frequently in the records as posing threats to public safety and the social order. There is no evidence, however, that they were any more likely than the average Spaniard to engage in rowdy behavior or to pose a threat to life and limb. Discriminated against and resentful of their treatment, some free blacks assaulted Spaniards on occasion. Such conduct, by no means the actions of the majority, led the authorities to attribute all manner of evil to the freed persons as a group. One Mexican viceroy, writing in 1590, observed that "in this land [Mexico] there is a large number of free Negroes and mulattoes who are so dangerous and pernicious, as is known, because they do nothing but gamble, loiter, and steal." Such observations reflected Spanish fears and prejudices, which prompted efforts to control and humiliate free blacks.

Very little is known about the texture of the lives of the free peoples of African descent in this early period or about the social institutions that they created. Scattered evidence suggests that as a group they were likely to choose their marriage partners from among their peers. Few males married slave women, probably because their children would take the mother's status. There was considerable interaction at other levels, however. Free blacks and slaves often belonged to the same *cofradías,* or mutual aid organizations, participated in conspiracies, established friendships, and worked together in *obrajes,* households, on sugar plantations, and so on.

The relationships of the free peoples with one another, however, was not always harmonious. There is some evidence that some of them adopted the racist views of Spanish society and gave a higher value to those who had a lighter skin color by virtue of a mixed ancestry. Some *cofradías* that free persons established in Lima, for example, admitted only mulattoes. Yet, in spite of such divisions, a similar heritage bound the free and the slave—a fact that none could forget. Slavery and discriminatory treatment in the Americas produced enormous stresses and strains in the lives of the freed people, but their common identity was never destroyed.

Few in number, but ever increasing, free blacks struggled to carve out a place for themselves in the societies of the Americas during the 16th century. The white colonists never passionately opposed their freedom, but freed blacks were never accorded all of the rights of full citizenship anywhere. Freed blacks were not owned by anyone, but an unfriendly white power structure still tried to treat them as if they were slaves. Their lot was never easy, but several of their number succeeded in acquiring skills, finding jobs, and accumulating property. They retained close ties with their kith and kin, who remained enslaved, recognizing that they had a common past and possibly a common future.

Negros.

CHAPTER 5
SHAPING AMERICA

The arrival of millions of Africans in the Americas from the 6th to the 19th centuries altered the human landscape forever. Although blacks formed a minority of the population at first, by the early 18th century they were in the majority in Brazil and in almost all of the Caribbean islands. They formed a much smaller share of the population in Mexico, Peru, Venezuela, and the rest of the Spanish colonies in Central and South America. There were about 400,000 slaves in English North America in 1750, a number that increased to about 4 million by 1860. The influence of African cultures could be seen everywhere in the Americas, but most dramatically in the Caribbean islands, Brazil, and in the United States.

The slave populations consisted of both African-born people and creoles. North America was the only society in this hemisphere where the slave population was able to sustain itself through natural increase. The fertility rate of the slave women in the societies of Latin America and the Caribbean was low—the consequence of poor diet, disease, overwork, and a population in which, at times, men outnumbered women by as much as 2 to 1 or 3 to 1. In addition, there was a very high infant mortality rate; babies fell victim to tetanus, gastroenteritis, and a number of diet-related disorders. Not until the 19th century, when medical

The purchases of African slaves are recorded in these ledgers and documents, and the silver used to make these coins was mined by slaves in Mexico. Despite being brought to the Americas against their will, African slaves and their descendants have had an immense influence on American societies.

knowledge and treatment began to improve, did some societies in Latin America and the Caribbean experience brief periods of natural increase in the slave populations.

For the black populations in the Americas, the 16th century represented the start of their unique historical odyssey. The estimated 300,000 Africans who arrived during that first century made crucial contributions to the shaping of the colonial societies. They also laid the foundations of the present-day black societies of the Americas. Whether they came in groups large or small, Africans brought their languages, religious beliefs, musical styles, cooking practices, and a thousand other aspects of their societies with them. Because Africans came from many different ethnic groups, they did not all share the same culture or ways of doing things. As a result, a variety of African beliefs and cultural forms went into the making and shaping of the societies of the Americas.

The distinctive cultural features of these societies, however, emerged slowly over time. Their formation depended on the size of the African population and the degree to which the people lived in large groups, thereby increasing social interaction and enhancing the prospect that much of their culture would be retained and transmitted to their children. If the members of one African ethnic group formed the majority in any one area, the culture that developed would, understandably,

African slaves cultivate sugarcane in the Caribbean. The labor of African slaves was indispensable in sugarcane cultivation and other agricultural enterprises in the Americas.

reflect their imprint. In general, however, the African slaves borrowed much from one another, and the American societies that they created drew upon many cultural roots.

Although their number was small at first, the labor of the Africans was indispensable in the mining industries, textile factories, and in sugar cultivation and other agricultural enterprises. By the second half of the 18th century, African workers had helped make sugarcane "king" in the Caribbean and Brazil. Vast numbers of slaves would by that time, or shortly thereafter, be used on the coffee plantations in Haiti and Brazil and in the cotton industry in the southern United States.

In terms of labor, African slaves made the principal contribution to the construction of the plantation economies of the Americas. But they were not the beneficiaries of their efforts. They formed an exploited labor force, and their energies went into the creation of wealth for those who owned them. Because they did not benefit materially from what they produced, the slaves really had no stake in the economic systems. Their labor was both forced and unpaid. Still, the roles that they played as workers in the building of the American societies must be recognized,

A sugar estate in Jamaica. Africans and their descendants helped build the foundations of present-day black societies of the Americas.

even as the slave systems that defined Africans and their children as property and tried to debase them at every turn should be condemned.

The economic benefits of slavery and the slave trade, even in the 16th century, went beyond the Americas. The European slave traders, slave owners, and their societies reaped economic rewards as well. These rewards increased as the slave trade and slavery expanded in the 17th and 18th centuries.

Starting in the 16th century, a number of European-produced goods—such as guns, textiles, woolen products, and pots and pans—were used in the African trade. The increased demand for these products benefited the economies of the areas that manufactured them. The construction of slave ships created jobs for carpenters, sail makers, painters, and other artisans. Slave traders brought African gold, ivory, and redwood back to Europe, imports that were in great demand. Then, too, the profits from the slave trade were frequently invested in other areas of the European economies.

Historians are not in agreement on the degree to which the slave trade was profitable. Several joint stock companies (corporations) went bankrupt in the first 200 years. But the independent traders who dominated the human traffic after about 1700 seemed to have done much better. The rate of profit or loss varied from trader to trader or from voyage to voyage. A great deal depended on the business sense and skills of the trader, the price of slaves on the African coast, their selling price in the Americas, the number who perished during the Atlantic crossing, and the state of their health upon arrival. With these qualifications in mind, most of the existing studies show a return of somewhere between 5 percent and 20 percent on the investment made by the traders. Some voyages could, of course, yield a higher return; others were a total disaster.

In the end, it may not be possible to separate the profitability of the slave trade from that of slavery. The two business practices were intricately interrelated. The funds that the slave trade generated were used to purchase the products that were produced with slave labor. Thus, a slave trader would sell his slaves in the Caribbean and use the funds to buy sugar, which he would then sell in Europe.

There are no reliable estimates of the returns that slave owners made on their investments in slaves in Latin America and the Caribbean. Investments in slaves in the United States in the 19th century yielded an

Fonthill Abbey, located in Wiltshire, England, was built with the profits made from a English family's sugarcane plantation in Jamaica. The profits from slavery and the slave trade were used in a variety of ways to improve life in Europe.

average rate of profitability of 10 percent, making for a very healthy business. Some Caribbean slave owners were heavily in debt by the beginning of the 19th century, but others must have continued to turn a profit. In fact, some scholars have argued that the profits from the slave trade and slavery played critically important roles in the growth of the European economies. The profits, according to these scholars, were invested in crucial enterprises, thereby generating economic growth. In other words, the economies of European countries, such as England, owed their expansion to the slave trade and the financial benefits of slave labor.

The impact of the slave trade on the African societies is also a highly controversial issue. Some scholars maintain that the removal of millions of people from West and West Central Africa led to the depopulation of certain societies. Others conclude that the African populations did not decline during the almost four centuries that the slave trade existed. They suggest that new food crops introduced during the period led to improved diets and helped to account for a steady increase in the population, even though millions were being drained away by the trade. These two points of view do not necessarily rule each other out.

The slave trade did not affect all African societies in the same way, and its impact varied over time. Some weaker societies disappeared, while the stronger ones with access to guns and gunpowder increased their power and size. They were able to incorporate other societies into their own, often selling the captives whom they took in the process. The fact that most of the slaves who were sold were young males must have had severe negative consequences in some societies. There were prob-

A Portuguese trading ship sets out from Lisbon for Brazil and the Caribbean. The slave trade helped expand European economies, creating jobs, increasing demand for manufactured goods, and providing investment funds for businesses.

This Benin bronze depicts a warrior chief with an assortment of weapons. The slave trade may have increased the incidence of warfare in Africa because of the availability of European weapons and the opportunity to trade prisoners for European manufactured goods.

ably imbalances in the number of men to women in some societies and a shortage of persons available for such male-assigned duties as defense.

The slave trade may also have increased the incidence of wars in the African societies. African societies in the 16th century and later went to war for their own local reasons. The popular view that the Europeans created wars between the Africans for the purpose of acquiring slaves is highly exaggerated. Nor is it generally true that the Africans fought primarily for the purpose of obtaining captives to be sold as slaves. It is very likely, however, that the availability of European-supplied weapons led to an increase in the frequency of wars. African societies that had access to these weapons of death were probably less willing to settle their

Part of the mural at the Palace of Cortés in Cuernavaca, Mexico, painted by artist Diego Rivera, depicts the descendants of African slaves taking part in the life of Mexico. Despite their enslaved condition, the Africans established cultural traditions that became the core of black life in the Americas.

disputes with others through negotiation. The captives could now be sold to the Europeans for more arms and consumer items. In time, many coastal states that traded extensively with the Europeans were able to exert power and control over their neighbors in the interior.

The slave trade, according to most scholars, had a negative economic effect on the African societies that were involved in it. This was because the Africans developed a taste for the consumer goods provided by the Europeans in exchange for the slaves. Because these goods could be obtained without undue difficulty and the prices were not excessive, some Africans developed a dependence on them and neglected their own local industries. In the long run, the Africans' failure to develop their own industries helps to account for their falling behind the Europeans in manufacturing. It should also be emphasized that the Africans exchanged their human victims for military or consumer products. These items did not contribute to the creation of wealth or to capital formation, as economists would describe it. On the other hand, the Europeans who purchased the Africans put them to work to create wealth. From a long-term economic standpoint, therefore, the Europeans got the better of the trading relationship.

The Atlantic slave trade left a lasting and bitter legacy for all groups involved in it. It has remained a source of embarrassment and guilt for them. Some have sought to establish blame and responsibility for its origins and continuation. The unpleasant fact is that there were African sellers and European and American buyers. The African sellers came from many different societies and so did the purchasers. The contemporary reader looks back in horror at human beings buying and selling other members of the human family. But most people at the time did not see anything wrong with the slave trade. Still, there were others, undoubtedly a small minority, who denounced the human traffic and reacted to it with disgust and disdain.

Blame and accusation aside, the extraordinary burdens that the enslaved endured must be recognized. They were human property, subjected to the whims of their owners, humiliated, and abused. As unfree workers, they labored long hours, often at dangerous tasks. Overworked and underfed, many died prematurely. Their life chances were limited, and few could expect to acquire their freedom. Yet, there is ample evidence that the enslaved called upon their inner strength to survive their ordeal. Beginning in the 16th century, they escaped and rebelled, challenging the power of those who denied them freedom. The enslaved everywhere established the cultural institutions that became the core of black life in the Americas. Theirs is a tale of extraordinary suffering; but it is also a timeless lesson in endurance and survival.

CHRONOLOGY

1441
Portuguese explorers capture Africans off the coast of Mauritania, signaling the start of a European trade in African slaves.

1444
Arrival of 235 to 240 kidnapped African slaves in Lisbon.

1479
Spain and Portugal sign the Treaty of Aláçovas, granting Portugal the right to supply the Spaniards with all the African slaves they needed.

1494
The first Africans arrive in Hispaniola with Christopher Columbus. They were free persons.

1502
African slavery introduced in Hispaniola, thereby inaugurating the institution in the Americas.

1511
Friar Antonio de Montesinos denounces the mistreatment of the Indians in Hispaniola.

1522
First rebellion by African slaves in the Americas occurs in Hispaniola.

1537
African slaves in Mexico conspire to rebel, but the plot is discovered.

1539
The black explorer Estevanico encounters the Zuni Indians in New Mexico and is killed.

1542
Spanish Crown abolishes Indian slavery and the *encomienda* system.

1550
First slaves to arrive in Brazil directly from Africa disembark at the city of Salvador.

1552
Revolt of slaves who work in the mines at Buria, Venezuela.

1559
Portuguese Crown issues a decree allowing the owners of sugar plantations in Brazil to import as many as 120 slaves for each sugar mill that they own.

1595
Spanish Crown awards the first *Asiento,* or monopoly contract, to supply the colonists with slaves.

1609
Runaway slaves in Mexico, led by Yanga, sign a truce with the Spaniards and obtain their freedom and a town of their own.

1612
Major slave conspiracy is discovered in Mexico City; 35 conspirators are executed.

1617
The town of San Lorenzo de los Negros receives its charter in Mexico, becoming the first officially recognized free settlement for blacks in the Americas.

1619
About 20 Africans disembark from a Dutch ship at Jamestown, Virginia.

GLOSSARY

AMANCEBADO
The state of concubinage, or unmarried couples living together

ASENTISTA
Person awarded an *Asiento*

ASIENTO
Monopoly contract awarded to traders by the Spaniards to supply African slaves to the colonies

BOZAL
Newly arrived African slave

CIMARRÓN
Runaway slave in Spanish America

COFRADÍA
Religious brotherhood

CRIOLLO
Person of African descent born in the Americas

ENCOMIENDA
Grant of Indian labor to a Spanish colonist

ENGENHO
Sugar mill (in Portuguese Brazil)

INGENIO
Sugar mill (in Spanish possessions)

LADINO
African slave acculturated to Spanish customs and culture

MAROON
Runaway slave in the English colonies

MARRON
Runaway slave in the French colonies

MESTIZO
Person of mixed Indian and Spanish ancestry

MITA
System of forced Indian labor for wages in Peru

MULATTO
Person of mixed Spanish and African ancestry

OBRAJE
Textile factory

QUILOMBO
Runaway slave community in Brazil

REPARTIMIENTO
System of forced and rotated Indian labor for wages in the Spanish colonies

ZAMBO
Person of mixed Indian and African ancestry

FURTHER READING

GENERAL AFRICAN-AMERICAN HISTORY

Bennett, Lerone, Jr. *Before the Mayflower: A History of Black America.* 6th rev. ed. New York: Viking Penguin, 1988.

———. *The Shaping of Black America.* New York: Viking Penguin, 1993.

Conniff, Michael, and Thomas J. Davis. *Africans in the Americas: A History of the Black Diaspora.* New York: St. Martin's, 1993.

Foner, Philip S. *History of Black Americans: From Africa to the Emergence of the Cotton Kingdom.* Westport, Conn.: Greenwood, 1975.

Franklin, John H., and Alfred A. Moss, Jr. *From Slavery to Freedom: A History of Negro Americans.* 6th ed. New York: Knopf, 1987.

Gates, Henry L., Jr. *A Chronology of African-American History from 1445–1980.* New York: Amistad, 1980.

Giddings, Paula. *When and Where I Enter: The Impact of Black Women on Race and Sex in America.* New York: Bantam, 1985.

Harding, Vincent. *There Is a River: The Black Struggle for Freedom in America.* San Diego: Harcourt Brace, 1981.

Hine, Darlene C., et al., eds. *Black Women in America.* Brooklyn, N.Y.: Carlson, 1993.

Meltzer, Milton. *The Black Americans: A History in Their Own Words.* Rev. ed. New York: HarperCollins Children's Books, 1984.

Mintz, Sidney W., and Richard Price. *The Birth of African-American Culture: An Anthropological Perspective.* Boston: Beacon, 1992.

Quarles, Benjamin. *The Negro in the Making of America.* 3rd ed. New York: Macmillan, 1987.

HISTORIES AND ACCOUNTS OF AFRICA AND THE AMERICAS

Curtin, Philip D., ed. *Africa Remembered: Narratives by West Africans from the Era of the Slave Trade.* Madison: University of Wisconsin Press, 1968.

Curtin, Philip D., Steven Feierman, Leonard Thompson, and Jan Vansina. *African History.* New York: Longman, 1978.

Knight, Franklin. *The Caribbean: The Genesis of a Fragmented Nationalism.* 2nd ed. New York: Oxford University Press, 1990.

Lockhart, James. *Spanish Peru, 1532–1560: A Colonial Society.* Madison: University of Wisconsin Press, 1967.

Lockhart, James, and Stuart Schwartz. *Early Latin America: A History of Colonial Spanish America and Brazil.* Cambridge and New York: Cambridge University Press, 1983.

Palmer, Colin A. *Slaves of the White God: Blacks in Mexico, 1570–1650.* Cambridge: Harvard University Press, 1976.

Rodney, Walter. *How Europe Underdeveloped Africa.* Rev. ed. Washington, D.C.: Howard University Press, 1982.

Rout, Leslie B. *The African Experience in Spanish America, 1502 to the Present Day.* Cambridge and New York: Cambridge University Press, 1976.

Schwartz, Stuart B. *Sugar Plantations in the Formation of Brazilian Society: Bahia 1550–1835.* Cambridge and New York: Cambridge University Press, 1986.

Thornton, John. *Africa and Africans in the Formation of the Atlantic World, 1400–1680.* Cambridge and New York: Cambridge University Press, 1992.

Van Sertima, Ivan. *They Came Before Columbus.* New York: Random House, 1976.

SLAVERY AND THE SLAVE TRADE

Bowser, Frederick P. *The African Slave in Colonial Peru, 1524–1650.* Stanford, Calif.: Stanford University Press, 1974.

Curtin, Philip D. *The Atlantic Slave Trade: A Census.* Madison: University of Wisconsin Press, 1972.

Davidson, Basil. *The African Slave Trade.* New York: Little, Brown, 1988.

Donnan, Elizabeth, ed. *Documents Illustrative of the Slave Trade to America.* 4 vols. Washington, D.C.: Carnegie Institution, 1930–35.

Equiano, Olaudah. *The Interesting Narrative of the Life of Olaudah Equiano, or Gustavus Vasa the African.* Edited by Paul Edwards. 2 vols. London: Heinemann, 1967.

Genovese, Eugene. *From Rebellion to Revolution: Afro-American Slave Revolts in the Making of the Modern World.* Baton Rouge: Louisiana State University Press, 1979.

Klein, Herbert. *African Slavery in Latin America and the Caribbean.* New York: Oxford University Press, 1986.

Lovejoy, Paul E. *Transformations in Slavery: A History of Slavery in Africa.* Cambridge and New York: Cambridge University Press, 1983.

Phillips, William D., Jr. *Slavery from Roman Times to the Early Atlantic Slave Trade.* Minneapolis: University of Minnesota Press, 1985.

Rawley, James A. *The Transatlantic Slave Trade.* New York: Norton, 1981.

Reynolds, Edward. *Stand the Storm: A History of the Atlantic Slave Trade.* Chicago: Ivan R. Dee, 1993.

Schwartz, Stuart B. *Slaves, Peasants, and Rebels: Reconsidering Brazilian Slavery.* Urbana: University of Illinois Press, 1992.

Watson, Alan. *Slave Law in the Americas.* Athens: University of Georgia Press, 1989.

INDEX

ACKNOWLEDGMENTS

This book was started and completed while I was an affiliated scholar at the Stanford Humanities Center during the academic year 1992–93. I would like to thank the director of the center, Wanda Corn; the associate director, Charles Junkerman; and the center's superb staff for their help and many courtesies. The University of North Carolina provided financial support, and I am extremely grateful for it. Leslie Lindzey deserves special thanks. She typed several drafts of the manuscript with her customary efficiency and good humor. Finally, the manuscript benefited from the wise counsel of the series editors, Robin Kelley and Earl Lewis. I remain deeply indebted to them.

Picture Credits

American Museum of Natural History, Department of Library Services (Neg. #329240): 64; Archivo General de la Nacion de Mexico: 76; Bancroft Library, University of California, Berkeley: 46; Bibliothèque Nationale, Paris: 93; British Library: 12 (Maps C.2.d.4), 14, 50, 111, 113; courtesy of the John Carter Brown Library at Brown University: 53; Werner Forman/Art Resource, New York: 22, 26, 115; Giraudon/Art Resource, New York: 54, 62, 98, 114; Hampton University Museum, Hampton, Virginia. Charles White, detail from *The Contribution of the Negro to Democracy in America,* 1943: 9; Library of Congress: 8, 29, 34, 39, 47, 59, 65, 67, 69, 91, 95, 105; the Mansell Collection, London: 28; Metropolitan Museum of Art: 19 (photography by Egyptian Expedition, neg. #TAA 178), 84 (the Crosby Brown Collection of Musical Instruments, 1889, #89.4.598); Museo de America, Madrid: 102; Museu Nacional de Arte Antiga, Lisbon: 23; National Maritime Museum, London: cover; New York Public Library, General Research Division, Astor, Lenox, and Tilden Foundations: 21, 79, 88; courtesy Peabody & Essex Museum, Salem, Mass.: 33; the Pierpont Morgan Library, New York. MA 3900, f.100: 42; Schalwijk/Art Resource, New York: 116; Schomburg Center for Research in Black Culture, New York Public Library, Astor, Lenox and Tilden Foundations: frontispiece, 35, 36, 37, 49, 52, 60, 66, 70, 71, 73, 75, 81, 83, 86, 110; Smithsonian Institution: 17 (Neg. #87-150); Maggie Steber: 108 (Casa de Moneda de Mexico, Archivo General de la Nacion de Mexico); original maps by Gary Tong: 20, 32, 44; University of Pennsylvania, the University Museum (Neg. #S5-23122): 10.

COLIN A. PALMER

Colin A. Palmer is Distinguished Professor of History at the Graduate School and University Center of the City University of New York. He was previously the William Rand Kenan, Jr., Professor of History at the University of North Carolina at Chapel Hill. There, he chaired the history department from 1986 to 1991 and also chaired African and Afro-American studies from 1980 to 1988. He is the author of several volumes about black history and slavery, including *Passageways: A History of Black America to 1865; Slaves of the White God: Blacks in Mexico, 1570–1650;* and the forthcoming *Africa's Children: The Pre-emancipation Experiences of Blacks in the Americas.* Professor Palmer has been a scholar at the Stanford Humanities Center and a fellow of the National Humanities Center.

ROBIN D.G. KELLEY

Robin D. G. Kelley is professor of history and Africana studies at New York University. He previously taught history and African-American studies at the University of Michigan. He is the author of *Hammer and Hoe: Alabama Communists during the Great Depression,* which received the Eliot Rudwick Prize of the Organization of American Historians and was named Outstanding Book on Human Rights by the Gustavus Myers Center for the Study of Human Rights in the United States. Professor Kelley is also the author of *Race Rebels: Culture, Politics, and the Black Working Class* and co-editor of *Imagining Home: Class, Culture, and Nationalism in the African Diaspora.*

EARL LEWIS

Earl Lewis is associate professor of history and Afroamerican studies at the University of Michigan. He served as director of the university's Center for Afroamerican and African Studies from 1990 to 1993. Professor Lewis is the author of *In Their Own Interests: Race, Class and Power in Twentieth Century Norfolk* and co-author of *Blacks in the Industrial Age: A Documentary History.*